A BOOK OF UNTRUTHS

MIRANDA DOYLE

A Book of Untruths

A Memoir

FABER & FABER

First published in 2017
by Faber & Faber Limited
Bloomsbury House
74–77 Great Russell Street
London WC1B 3DA

Typeset by Faber & Faber Limited
Printed in the UK by CPI Group (UK) Ltd, Croydon, CR0 4YY

Photographs on pp. 96, 106, 107, 109, 120 by Tom Kidd and on
p. 187 by Sarah Jackson. All other images courtesy of the author.

Every effort has been made to trace or contact all copyright holders.
The publishers would be pleased to rectify any omissions or errors
brought to their notice at the earliest opportunity.

A CIP record for this book
is available from the British Library

ISBN 978–0–571–33166–6

FSC
www.fsc.org
MIX
Paper from
responsible sources
FSC® C020471

2 4 6 8 10 9 7 5 3 1

In memory
of Mum and Dad,
John Francis and Maureen Helen.
You were always more loving and more complex
than I have been able to write.

In talking about the past, we lie with every breath we draw.

William Maxwell, *So Long,*
See You Tomorrow

1st June 2006
  Miranda
You have my
full permission
 to write anything
  you want Mum

Lie 1: I didn't do it

What is the first lie? Often so much is grafted to deceit in the telling, that afterwards the layers are difficult to unpick. So let's start with a straightforward lie. A lie of omission. It's as good an introduction as any to each of the players of our story – my family of six.

It's the end of the day, and four children stand on the brand new textured linoleum of a seventies kitchen, hands clasped tight over their bums.

There is a smell of smoke and paraffin, an unsightly burn tarnishing Mum's new floor. The lino pattern was her choice. Orange flowers, bordered by a fake wooden square, now repeat across the vast space between me and the back door. The man came to put it down last week.

Dad strides the length of us. Adrian, my eldest brother, is a teenager and his own mother dead. Blond, freckled and lanky, he is as remote as stone. Sean, adopted, is dark-haired, dark-eyed, and at twelve is the kind of child dubbed 'enthusiastic' and 'energetic' by his teachers, and 'completely out of hand' by every other mother we know. Next is me, the token girl. Aged six, I have red hair, wonky teeth and an eye that drifts when it's tired. Finally there is round-faced, red-lipped Ed, who can only be four. Like Paddington he eats marmalade neat from the spoon, his stomach white and taut as a drum.

'Who did it?' Dad bawls.

Dad is a lecturer in Maths at Heriot-Watt University in Edinburgh. He's dragged himself through poverty and prejudice to get here, and the difficulties are still not behind him. A father of four, he has lost one wife to septicaemia and gained a second, completing his PhD in the evenings, between bouts of Open University marking and the kind of parenting we find him in the midst of here.

I try to edge backwards, but am prevented by the kitchen table, where it is beached on a section of serviceable brown carpet tiles. It is this table we are hostage to twice each day, stuck in close proximity to a father whose unhappiness reminds me of the kind of fury the barking dog at the brewery shows, dragging its chain.

In memory it is not clear whether that day Mum has already lost the plot over the burnt lino and Dad arrives into this panic. More likely he brings it with him. A quiet, internal panic that drums through me till I can think of nothing else.

Most evenings I'm alert to the way the front door opens, and how long the silence lasts once our father is in the hall. I know about the density of traffic on Lothian Road, the vagaries of the head of department, and the difficulties of parking on the High Street outside. Sometimes, towards six o'clock, I peer through the fugged-up windows at the fifteen car-parking spaces on the harbour front, fingers crossed.

But burnt lino is far, far worse than inadequate parking and trouble at work. It is so bad my head is a white-hot hell.

'Who did it?'

The answer is obvious. It seems impossible, even now, to think that Dad would have gone through the pantomime of asking. Yet he asks it again:

'Who did it?'

My mother, in early memory, is like a mum in a cartoon: with her back to me, shackled to the white goods. Her loyalties are with the other adult. The scary one. The one shouting so loud the whole street will hear.

My loyalties must be with my elder brothers. They demand it. It is this fealty that silences the moist kitchen, condensation thick on every window, bubble and squeak in the pot. The stink of cabbage and corned beef mingles with the overwhelming stench of paraffin and burn.

'Who did it?'

Dad knows who did it. Everyone knows. Because the steam engine has only been in the house as long as the lino. It is an inappropriate present to Ed, that Sean covets, and that we'll never, ever see again.

However, for once Sean has not destroyed something on purpose. That's why he hesitates. The burn is an accident. An honest mistake.

Nobody speaks.

Till Ed can stand it no longer. His weakness is terrible and empowering: as soon as one of us has given in to terror, the rest of us can feel better that we didn't.

It's not a feeling-better that will last. The noise Ed makes begins to fill every corner of me, the anxiety brimming up

3

inside like sickness. From experience I know my little brother's cry will make things worse. Dad may not wait for an answer. He may go right ahead and beat us all.

But thankfully he makes a break for it, dragging Sean through the kitchen by his ear. He does not wait to get him up the stairs to his schoolmaster's belt, but thrashes him right there in the hall, with the one that was buckled round his own trousers. And all I can think is that this is all Ed's fault.

Lie 2: I am lying

Since this is a book about lying let's start off with some facts.

We all do it. Politicians, of course, are amongst the worst. There's Watergate, the Clinton blowjob, Blair's confused attitude to the evidence on the eve of the war in Iraq. Widespread institutional deception plagues the front pages. Individually and collectively we've been brought to our knees by the deceit of bankers. There's the shameful behaviour of the Catholic Church as it tried to protect its reputation, and the scramble by the police to save themselves after the Hillsborough Stadium disaster of 1989.

Police themselves are lied to every day. In one study by the Innocence Project, more than 25 per cent of wrongfully convicted people had made a false confession. People lie to keep themselves out of prison, but they also lie to end interrogations orientated around the presumption of dishonesty. Lies beget lies.

4

Findings show that the bigger the brain, the more frequent the deceit. Lemurs are less sneaky than chimpanzees. Humans lie most. Those who are interested in lie detection estimate that the average person will lie three times within a few minutes of meeting a stranger, and between ten and two hundred times a day. Women are more likely to lie to make the person they are talking to feel good, while men most often lie to make themselves look better.

Whether we're a ten-a-day fibber or tell a monstrous two

5

hundred, fMRI scans show that, when we do it, the prefrontal cortex is active. The prefrontal cortex is a little like Putin's FSB – preoccupied with conflict, error detection, risky decisions and executive control. It also has a capacity, like the FSB's director of records and archives, to retrieve those remote memories that we may wish were long forgot.

The reason the prefrontal cortex is the site of deceitfulness, rather than the more ancient, routine areas of the brain, is that telling a lie requires twice as much effort as being honest. We must weigh what we want to hide, build a deceitful version behind which to hide it, give a convincing performance, and finally remember that lie for the rest of our lives.

Research from the University of Southern California shows that structural brain abnormalities develop in people who habitually lie. Pathological liars have significantly more 'white matter' than 'grey matter' in their prefrontal lobe.

Grey matter is thought.

White matter is the communicative equipment between cells, or the wiring between thoughts.

This white matter is what gives liars a natural advantage. Habitually telling lies is an effort, an effort that thought – grey matter, or the worry, guilt and regret that we experience when we fib – inhibits. Researchers call the experience of these emotions 'cognitive load'. Cognitive load is stress on the brain's power to manage itself.

Paul Ekman, the psychologist who pioneered research into how emotions relate to our facial expressions, argues that this cognitive load leads to 'leakage'. Leakage happens in the hands and the feet. Their movements betray us. The face we control with more vigilance. Chamberlain was to say when Hitler promised not to invade Czechoslovakia: 'I got the impression that here was a man who could be relied upon when he had given his word.' It would be another few decades before we learned that psychopaths don't leak.

Psychopaths are in a league of their own when it comes to lying. A study in 2009 found that they were two and a half times more likely than their saner counterparts to be granted parole. One could argue that this is less about having a better control of their deceit and more about self-belief. But for those of us who are not psychopaths, cognitive load is about the anxiety that we will leak and therefore be discovered.

Researchers at the University of Notre Dame asked 110 people to take a lie-detector test every week for ten weeks, reporting how many lies they had told. By the end of the study, all the subjects lied less, and all reported improvements in their relationships and sleep patterns; they had fewer headaches and fewer sore throats.

Liars talk too much, as you may have noticed. They bury their lies in narrative. Sometimes they use the third person, slipping from I into s/he, which enables them to disown their deceit, and they swear more than most. The amount of self-policing that goes into controlling a lie creates a situation where other areas of presentation fall out of control. For instance we may lumber into incoherence, repetition, aggression and pointing fingers. Liars also make better lie detectors. Individuals who are good at lying are good at catching others out.

For the majority of us it's hard to detect a falsehood. On the whole we're a gullible species, tending to think the best of one another. Our rate of lie detection is extremely poor, statistically only slightly greater than chance. Scientists call this a truth bias. When we are lied to by those we trust, the truth bias accentuates the betrayal we feel. As a result the cost to the liar is often enormously high. We may think that Tony Blair has got away with murder, and a small fortune besides, but when Boris Johnson, of all people, feels comfortable calling him an 'epic, patronising tosser', the short-term gains of Blair's refusal to differentiate between self-belief and certitude must be a position he regrets. Though history may contest the versions of Blair's leadership there can be no dispute that his mendacity let us down.

This version of a life will be contested too.

However, I have not set out to deceive you. I want to tell you my story as truthfully as I can. But I must warn you, I have lied on occasion too.

Philosophers talk about a Liar Paradox. The statement 'I am lying' is impossible to unravel and is an area of logic which, after 2,300 years, still remains unresolved. 'I am telling the truth' will have its significant difficulties too.

But here, between these pages, I promise that I really, really will.

Lie 3: It's an ulcer

Pat is Adrian's mum and after she died Dad swept the house clear of her. Then he found another – mine.

My eldest brother was a blond, blue-eyed child with freck-

les dotting his nose, and to Pat he was perfect. The only child she wanted. After Adrian there could be no other man. And there wasn't. She died on 30 April 1965 at St Bartholomew's Hospital, Rochester. She was twenty-nine years old.

I believed in the ulcer and I'm sure my own mother did too. The 'private doctor' we bought into wholesale. It wasn't until Dad had died that the euphemism was pointed out. Ulcers were how women communicated an unwanted pregnancy, and it is only as I write this that I wonder whether the lie was not Dad's but Pat's. She insisted on getting rid of 'it', he would say when he spoke of the ulcer. She'd organised the operation herself.

There are only a few photographs of Adrian's mother remaining. In these she is a thin, pale woman, with anxiety twisting her mouth. Pictured together with Dad in their marriage photo, to me there is an intangibility about her,

9

as though she were an empty dress, my gaze drawn away to the man beside her.

When they married Dad gave Pat pearls. Pearls are sorrow, my grandmother told him, and after Pat died he stored them, like guilt, beneath the bed.

There was never a time that we did not know of Adrian's loss, and there was never a time that we spoke of it. Her death was only noted in reference to Dad's renunciation of the Catholic Church. It wasn't the ulcer that had killed her, he would say, but the belief 'in everything a priest says'.

Adrian had arrived in May 1960. It was a difficult birth. Another pregnancy, the midwife told Pat, would mean death, a prognosis that would come to be a curse. Adrian's mother took her Catholic faith seriously, and in consultation with the priest, came up with a fatal compromise: no more babies.

Contraception was never mentioned. God knew better than any doctor, the priest had told them without irony. Life and death were his game.

Without the priest's blessing there could be no sex. Dad found himself derailed by one of those Catholic dilemmas where a mother's mortality is weighed against a baby's, and a husband's sanity never comes into it at all.

However, for the creative-minded, there are always solutions. Church ethicists have a Get Out of Jail Free card for this kind of bind, called 'double effect'. Double effect allows unintended bad consequences (for instance, the use of a condom) to be annulled when weighed against the pursuit of good (the saving of Pat's life). Then in order to offset any sinful preventative action Dad decided that he would adopt. Adoption was a nod to the thorny issue of

Catholic procreation. To adopt was to have more children without killing his wife.

In 1963 they adopted a baby boy: Sean.

Soon after, we were told, an ulcer grew in Pat's stomach. Was it Dad's anger that caused it? Or her being forced to mother a hyperactive child that she had never asked for? Or was it simply a question of intercourse: did Pat, fearing for her life, decide to have the ulcer removed?

When Adrian was five, and Sean two, she booked herself in for a private operation from which she never returned. Pat died of septicaemia within days of leaving theatre and it wasn't till Dad was dying himself that he admitted the regret he felt over paying the bill.

Like the lavish three-string circle of pearls, Pat soon disappeared, her pictures and belongings secreted into shoeboxes, away from Adrian's gaze.

Yet ever after Pat would haunt us all.

Lie 4: You've beated me to it

It was never hidden from Sean that he was adopted. He was reminded of it most days. He's the cuckoo in our nest, adopted in 1963 from a Catholic orphanage; there is a sense that in the sixties parents were not closely vetted. John Francis – Dad – was just the kind of man they were looking for. He and his wife attended Mass.

Often Sean tells me of his wish. What he wishes is that on the day Dad came looking for proof that babies are always a blessing, his infant self had been aloud and awake. Yet on that summer morning, to his regret, my father found him asleep.

Rather like dog and cat homes now, Dad was shown rooms and rooms of caged beds. The place was as noisy as Battersea. Except for one gorgeous black-haired baby, lying on his tummy, fist curled up by his cheek. The nun, Dad told me years later, held nothing back in her long list of reservations. Sean, as the baby had been named, was sickly. And difficult.

Sean's grandmother was French, and in Sean's cot, be-

side him, was the pale-blue sitty-up bear she had sent him, which perhaps he still has. For me this bear is proof of other possibilities, and of the terrible weight of chance.

He used his bear for our sex education, making an inch-long slice through the abdomen. Sometimes the bear was a girl, and sometimes, when his stuffing leaked out, Sean moulded it into a pale frazzled penis. Then she became a boy.

The adoption can only have been my father's decision. When he talked of that day and the sleeping baby, there was never any mention of his first wife.

Sean tells me Dad would say before a beating:

'If you carry on like this, you'll go back to the home,' or, 'Adrian's mother never wanted you,' or, 'I only adopted you because Adrian was getting spoiled.'

Sean's own mother, the biological one, would grow to be a fantasy parent to each one of us. She was the mother I dreamed about, probably as much as Sean did himself.

Eventually in the eighties she was located. The Southern Catholic Rescue Society had been her rescuer, and it was they who were able to find his mother again.

Mary was young when she gave birth to Sean, and from Folkestone. His father was a twenty-one-year-old Persian Muslim student called Esse, who returned to Iran. He has been impossible to locate.

In Sean's brown envelope, where he keeps the proof of who he is, there is, amongst the bits and pieces, a certificate of baptism, without godparents, and a list of possible contenders for the role of mother. The list is written in pencil and includes Marys who have been found in Southend, Newcastle, East Glamorgan, Manchester and Crewe.

The social worker writes a long letter to him with advice on contact, in which Sean is counselled to use the words 'looking for family' rather than 'mother'. She fears that the wrong person could get hold of the correspondence. It has happened before. She wonders whether it might be better to get the priest to call round, which has the advantage of being 'perhaps a little more delicate in terms of catching [Mary] on her own'.

Once the introduction is made, Mary writes that she always had 'every intention of getting in touch' but Sean had 'beated' her to it. After he calls, she writes to him that she 'cannot always answer questions'. She worries that she will be overheard. 'We must be very careful. I must not upset the apple cart just yet.'

The word 'yet' implies a future. But with Mary there has been none. Though Sean has called round to her house, apple carts still stand in his way. He is a truth that Mary has never had the courage to confess. His half-siblings have no clue that he is here.

Lie 5: I'm number three

Mum often mentioned the baby conceived before me. It died in the womb at thirty-four weeks. It wasn't until I was pregnant myself that she told me the midwife had not allowed her to see the child, or to know its sex. Her firstborn was taken to the hospital incinerator, neatly wrapped in a plastic bag.

My arrival was ghosted by grief for this child she never saw. A child that, to her, also represented life's vengeful balance. Every action had a consequence. One life must be given for another. It wasn't until after my father was dead that she told me of her very first baby, the one that had come before the dead one. The one she felt she had not been able to have.

The night they met, Dad had been a widower less than a year. He was six foot, and an attractive man in his thirties, with two small boys. If it hadn't been for the fact he had come from an Irish single-parent family, women would have been queuing round the block. The single parent, my grandmother, was much in evidence during those early months, helping with the boys, her corset stinking of cabbage and cigarettes and the biscuity underside of old woman. To see her was to know what lay in store.

They met at a Territorial Army event where ladies were at a premium. My mother had been invited to swell the numbers, with a party of friends she had made at secretarial

college. They shared a flat, loved the Beatles, and had spent the previous summer hanging out with The Scaffold at the Edinburgh Fringe. It was the sixties, and the county set of Edinburgh were doing their best to catch up.

She was the only daughter of a Protestant mill owner based in Tillicoultry. As soon as her parents got wind of the affair they dispatched her to London, and a job at the British Medical Association, hoping danger would pass.

It didn't. In need of a mother for his children, and a wife for his bed, my father remained focused. He hung around outside her office in Chelsea with flowers on Fridays, though it was six and a half hours by train from Waverley to King's Cross.

One weekend Dad described arriving to find a house party in full swing. Aside from his toothbrush, he had with him only a full bottle of gin, which he stingily hid in the oven. It brought the party to an explosive climax in the small hours when one of her flatmates decided to warm up a quiche.

On one of these visits he got Mum pregnant.

There was an appointment in Harley Street, she told me. Again Dad paid.

It was still a couple of years before legalised abortion. However, my mother would have felt there was no other choice. Shotgun weddings were not an option in Perthshire. The worst of it was that it would have proved her parents' bigotry – John Doyle, as a poor Irish Catholic, was absolutely the wrong man.

You would think that abortion could lead to other choices, but guilt was the glue that kept them together. The termination sealed her fate.

Cine footage of their marriage shows a small marquee has been erected in the paddock. Granny, dressed in orange, is so drunk she leans into the camera as if into a stiff wind. Granddad has remained indoors, in tears.

Lie 6: I looked it up on Google

A short while after Dad's death I told Mum about research I'd read, which suggested that a stressful pregnancy often leads to a tearful baby. We were standing on the stairs, the house filled with my own baby's screams.

'Did any of *us* cry?' I asked.

'Ed cried.'

Of course he did. When he was small and podgy and pale, this youngest blue-eyed boy, with marmalade hair, cried loads. Really cried. The rest of us would rather die than give in to tears, but Ed rolled over as soon as he was poked. Maybe the reason he is so serene now is that he blew it all out of himself before the age of five.

The staircase was dark as Mum and I spoke, the baby quieting against my shoulder.

'I was ill during your brother's pregnancy,' she said.

'Something serious?'

'We were told Ed would lose his sight.' There was a long pause while she weighed the balance of things. 'It was something your father gave me.'

'Something he gave you?' There was another pause. 'What did he give you?'

'Grounds for divorce.'

It did not take me as long to process this answer as it should have.

'An STD?'

She didn't reply, the baby huffing hot breaths against my neck.

'A sexually transmitted disease?' I squeaked. 'An STD?' This was a woman who waved her hands above her head in church each Sunday morning. 'Which one?'

And this was a woman who had never to my knowledge slept with any other man. Watching her continue her way quietly down the staircase, I stood on my step a long, long time.

When I cornered her in the kitchen later she said she didn't know which STD.

'Come on.' I wanted to believe her. 'Hepatitis and herpes you'd know about, because you can't get rid of them.'

One beautiful flatmate of mine, in the midst of a flare-up, would spend a good deal of her time in a salted bath, feeling disgraced.

I tackled Mum again.

'My God, you must know. What medication did they give you?'

'They gave me some pills,' she said.

'And told you there was a risk of infant blindness?' Dad must have spent the rest of the pregnancy holding his breath. 'Well that's gonorrhoea or syphilis, isn't it? But you'd remember if it was syphilis? You'd have to remember that?'

When still she wouldn't answer I asked:

'Who did he catch it off?'

She looked away.

'He went to one of your uncle's parties,' she said. 'He was drunk.'

'And?'

I still couldn't quite believe her. I wanted proof.

'Perhaps they visited a prostitute,' she said.

I was not quite speechless:

'Was it the clap?'

'You seem to know a good deal about sexually transmitted diseases.'

Though I did, I told her I'd Googled it.

'It must have been the clap,' I said into the silence. 'I mean gonorrhoea causes blindness and when treated goes away. That must be it, mustn't it?'

She gave me a weary look.

'If you say so.'

I briefed Ed some months later. If it were me, I told myself, I'd want to know. Really, really want to know. Without realising that knowing some things can feel like ruin.

I got it off my chest in the car on the way to a ferry. It was a few days after Christmas and as I spoke, a service station strayed into view on his right-hand side. Without a word

Ed pulled in. I watched as he filled the tank with petrol and strolled into the shop to pay. He was gone many, many minutes, I stewing in the front seat. When he returned to the car he said nothing. Absolutely nothing. It was a silence I could only have breached at huge cost, and I didn't.

Lie 7: Memoir is non-fiction

Derived from the French, the word 'memoir' is an amalgam of the masculine *le mémoire* – 'a written record' – and the feminine *la mémoire* – 'memory' – and as a genre, like memory itself, memoir is always biased and open to distortion. In some cases it is entirely false.

It is only these active lies that we hear about – the autobiographical hoax, such as James Frey's *A Million Little Pieces* or Misha Defonseca's *Misha: A Mémoire of the Holocaust Years*. These are lies that are reported in the broadsheets, and their authors hung out to dry. Oprah Winfrey, when she interviewed Frey a second time, used the word 'duped'.

Frey was shamed because the contract between a memoirist and his or her reader is honesty. It is all that stands between autobiography dissolving into fiction and being put out to pulp.

The crime Frey committed was lying about the facts. It was a conscious premeditated act, like murder, and its perpetrator deserved to be punished. The other kind of deceit that a memoirist faces – nudging a life into shape so that it will read better – is not the same thing at all.

Some critics find autobiographies morally suspect. In the past in order to write a memoir you had to have done something worthwhile. Whereas today, one journalist writing in the *New York Times* tells us that the genre has been 'disgorged by virtually everyone who has ever had cancer', watched a parent die, or ridden a bike. In fact memoirists are not writers, but sadists who submit the reader to the underwhelming and the banal.

Admittedly cancer will come up here, some parents do die and there is even mention of a bike. My apologies. Neither have I done anything worthwhile. Perhaps then the answer is to drop the 'memoir' label and throw myself in with 'creative non-fiction'. Here truth is no longer the measure. Anything underwhelming can be overcome by imagination. Or is creative non-fiction really just an excuse to lie?

And I don't want to lie.

Yet even if we sincerely want to tell the truth, whatever the genre, there will be a layer of deceit that none of us can be conscious of. Our brains are not answerable to the reader, or to the self. Every day the cerebral cortex creates new neural pathways and alters existing ones, pruning, strengthening. Our memories are in a state of impermanence. If, as scientists say, our brains are plastic then our memories must be too.

Remote memories are retrieved and collated in the prefrontal cortex, the neural network from where lies spring. Like a lie, which is adapted over time to suit the listener, so is memory honed with every retelling. If the prefrontal cortex governs both deceit and remembering it may not be too wild a suggestion to imagine that these two functions overlap.

We do not conceive of ourselves through the lies we tell, but through the memories that stack up in our past. Without this library to refer to, we would have no sense of who we are. Our selves consist merely of a collection of moments, which we try to cohere through narration. We attempt to make permanent what is not. Like lying, memory is a process of (re)construction. When we remember, we assemble the fragments together, filling in the gaps with expectation and assumption. We construct our memories, in the same way that we build a lie.

It was in these gaps that Elizabeth Loftus, a researcher specialising in false memory, was able to convince a quarter of her study participants that they had been lost as a child in a shopping centre when they absolutely had not. False memories, she argues, arise from external suggestion and 'imagination inflation'. When we are hoaxed, as in the lost-in-the-mall scenario, we begin to believe. To construct.

And construction is essential for this genre. To write a life the author must organise memory into an inauthentic linear structure, selecting only what fits. As she writes she adapts her narrative to suit the perceived reactions of those she is writing for, and the more she sharpens her story the more convincing she will feel.

Let me be plain then. I have lied just as much as I need to. I have written up dialogue that I can no longer remember, cut characters I don't need, changed names because I have been ordered to, and generally neatened up a fractured and disjointed life. The narrative, in the end, will be as flawed as its narrator. A narrator who, when she says she has set out to unravel the 'truth', can only be described as deluded. Because in refracting the past through deceit, I could never have anticipated that there would be so many lies nor that so many would be my own.

Lie 8: Happy families

If we were to assign character roles, there is no question that Mum, Maureen Helen, is our victim.

What I remember most is how she smelled. The empty sharpness of her breath when she licked her finger to remove food stains from my face, and the Anaïs Anaïs she squirted, eyes closed. This girly, floral scent was an antidote to the totem bottles of Chanel No. 5 that lined the bathroom shelf. Each one a guilt gift from Dad that she never opened.

Mum must have struggled, in the years after I was born, to define her self at all. A stepmother at twenty-three, she had fallen from a life of personalised number plates and complaints about the 'help' into penury and tedium. The stepchildren didn't like her, her husband couldn't keep himself to himself, and each Sunday, when she trailed back to Perthshire to check in on her old life, her parents reminded her what a horrible mistake she had made.

The Patersons owned a woollen factory that her elder brother would later allow to drift into bankruptcy. He inherited, too, the house with its turret, stables, lodge houses and acres of farmland, and although there were portraits and land-

scapes disappearing from the walls, it was always made clear that if we were going to emulate anything then this was it. These people were descended from a long line of women who had 'come out' to kings and queens.

Born for privilege, Mum was mothered by a series of nannies – unhappy nannies, incompetent nannies, and nannies who refused to iron. As early as possible, she was banished to boarding school, an exile from which she never came home.

Mum told me about a workshop she had attended with a group of Christians in Glasgow. The discussion had deteriorated into competing stories over who had had the lousiest childhood.

'Well,' she piped up when there was a lull in proceedings, 'I was raised by nannies.'

'The only nanny I ken', said an older woman into the silence, 'is a goat.'

It was always a bit of a trial to Mum that her privilege denied her any adequate sympathy. And it's true, the kinds of complaints she and I might make, about boarding schools and maternal neglect, are patently embarrassing when set against poverty, illness, war.

However, there was often a sense that her parents just didn't like her. She was a girl. Her elder brother had no need, thanks to primogeniture, to worry on that score, and the younger was a sweet-natured man who brought out the best in his parents. Both siblings had married well.

Even so, each Sunday we'd drive north along the A7 to the Paterson estate where we were reminded what it was she had forsaken. There was sherry and Sunday lunch, lovingly prepared by Mrs McGregor, the last stalwart 'help' my grandmother ever had. Sometimes there was croquet on the lawn, or we children were dispatched to pick raspberries, or play, without irony, the only card games Granny possessed – Happy Families and Old Maid – followed by afternoon tea – drop scones and cake, served on a shiny trolley.

The enmity between my grandparents and Dad meant that heading home to Edinburgh we, on the back seat, would moan about the cheap Izal loo paper in the downstairs lavatory. It was the only example we could find that might make Mum and Dad feel better about the choices they had made.

Lie 9: It's people crying that puts Dad in a bad mood

It is Shrove Tuesday and Ed is still in his high chair. Not a high chair that holds him in, but a chair with long legs like a spider, so that he can reach his plate. We are all patient. If everyone is good there will be pancakes for tea. So we are. I don't even suck my thumb.

The living room, where the television is and where guests sit, is in the front of the house, but we are in the back. The kitchen dangles out into the garden beside us like a tube. To get out the back door we have to squeeze past Mum, who's always at the stove or the sink, past Trudy our poodle, the food bowl, the rubbish bin and the welly boots.

In this room the walls are dark. Really dark. Mum and Dad painted them to help baby Ed sleep; he never did when he was little. Someone told them that they should put him in the farthest corner of the house and leave him. They did that too.

Where Ed had to cry himself to sleep is not a dining room, like the posh one Granny has. It's just a place to eat, with five chairs, a high seat, the table, a dresser covered in post, homework, school bags, tools, toys. Ed doesn't have to sleep here any more. He sleeps in my room and I'm in the top bunk. Sean is in a bunk bed too, in the room next to ours. Adrian is in the attic. Adrian doesn't allow Ed and me into the attic. We are only allowed to stand in the doorway where we admire his papier-mâché train world of tunnels and hills. Ed loves how the engines whirr round and round in circles, but I don't think the view of the trains is very good from the door. I look out the attic window to the roof-tops and the sky. As I watch the birds balance on the neighbour's aerial I think my eldest brother has a very different life.

Apart from meal times when he has to be here, Adrian isn't. Maybe because Dad is angry all the time. Sean has lit fires on the stair carpet, and complaints have been made by the neighbours. He has been seen, like Spiderman, on the upstairs window ledge, scaling the house from outside. The belt is out a lot. Adrian got it for crashing his bicycle and when Dad caught my fingers in the car door I got walloped too. Not with the belt, because we were at Blackford Pond.

Dad takes us there every Saturday to feed the ducks. Sean falling into the duck pond definitely puts Dad in a bad mood, because Sean's done that more than once.

Maybe what Dad hates is if we cry. Not that Sean cries, even if he gets soaked in the pond. Ever.

Today is okay though. There will be no crying or falling into ponds. There are pancakes. The door to the kitchen is open. My parents stand in full view, an argument brewing. My stomach grows tight with it. Maybe there will be no pancakes after all, even though we are being so good. We have been really, really good since lunchtime because of the pancakes. Even Sean.

Soon Dad is filling the mouth of the kitchen door.

'I've just bet your mum fifty pounds that I can toss the best pancake.'

Fifty pounds! Does he not know that Mum's spent a year at finishing school, where the only things she learned were how to toss pancakes and how to get out of a car without putting her knickers on show? Fifty pounds. It is so much money that Mum could fill the bath right the way up to the top with halfpenny chews.

Sean is already off his seat to see. Adrian follows. Ed is clambering down from his chair too. Dad does not seem to be mad about them getting down, though they haven't asked. In fact he seems happy. Maybe he wants us all to watch him win.

Dad goes first, like he's going to show us all how it's done. His confidence eases my stomach ache.

Fifty pounds. He cannot lose.

Things are going well until the toss. The toss is difficult, a game-changing time with pancakes. Everything is at stake. But the batter is not lifting as easily as it should. Dad is shoogling the pan, attacking it with the fish slice.

Pancake finally free, he announces he's ready to go. Showing off, he flicks the pan so hard that the pancake hits the ceiling. We watch as it falls, then slumps back into the pan, half on, half off, torn, a mess.

If Granddad had hit the ceiling with a pancake it would be funny, but when Dad does it nobody laughs. Ed, edging between our legs, is too dwarfed by the rest of us to see the greasy ceiling or the tangled pancake on the stove.

My stomach ache is back. But it's okay because Mum will know not to win. She'll know that she can't.

She carelessly wipes the pan with more oil, ladling the batter in. She swirls it out to form a large round disc.

Dad has been giving a speech about going first being an unfair handicap, but now we all watch.

Mum nibbles the edges of it with the fish slice, shakes the pan, watching it slide easily back and forth over the surface. Then she flicks her wrist. A tidy toss, an elegant turn over in mid-air that lands the pancake back directly from where it took off.

I close my eyes. It is a decisive win, for which we are all going to pay.

Ed says loudly into the silence:

'Who won?'

My stomach flips. If anything's going to make it worse it is this. Someone jabs his arm. Perhaps it is me.

'Mum won,' Dad says spinning round. 'Mum did.' He isn't pointing his finger, and he's not gritting his teeth. 'And now she's going to make all the pancakes,' he tells us. 'Just this once she's been better at it than me.'

No one reminds him that she has also won fifty pounds. We

are confused over what has just happened, but not insane. Mum wipes the pan again with oil and ladles the batter in.

'Who wants the next one?' she asks.

As I clamber back onto my chair I think they must be playing a different game.

Lie 10: He married well

All of us cheat.

When I asked my husband, who has been known to cheat at Risk, how cheating counts as winning, he said:

'Winning's got nothing to do with it. It's about not losing.'

A more nuanced friend pointed out that losing at Snakes and Ladders, a game of chance, is tolerable, but losing at Scrabble or chess is not. Anything is fair to avoid intellectual defeat.

How we play games tells us a lot about our personality, traits that often remain with us our entire lives. Are we bad losers, cheaters, furiously competitive, saboteurs or rule bores? Scientists at North Eastern University in Massachusetts are developing the Virtual Personality Assessment Laboratory, where their aim is to reveal the authentic personalities of participants through play. It is, they argue, a much better indicator than a simple job interview, because candidates are not thinking 'I should do this to make myself look better.' All they are interested in is winning. To me there was never any point. It was always more straightforward to lose.

Contemporary theorists who study cheating have steered away from thinking that there are principled people and unprincipled people. They would suggest that we weigh up the situation. The loss. The gain. Then make a decision. For instance, we are more likely to cheat in a darkened room than a fully lit one. The more powerful we feel the more likely we are to indulge ourselves, too – just sitting in a bigger car, which boasts a more expansive seat, is a good predictor of how likely we are to try to get away with it, pushing in at crammed motorway exits and running the lights. We cheat more in a messy environment, picking up on the chaos and the deviance. We also cheat more when we believe ourselves to be on our own. Therefore it should always be good policy, when we go to the lav, to take our Monopoly money with us.

Psychologists have found that children who have a reputation to maintain are less likely to double-cross. Poor Sean was so ground down and in despair over his reputation he must have wagered that there was nothing to be gained by honesty. It took Ed and me months to realise Sean had creased the Old Maid card in Granny's pack.

A close friend, who supports children with educational needs, talks of their emotional landscape in terms of poker chips. When good things happen they win more chips, and when bad things happen they lose them. Many kids are so out of chips that they cannot afford to lose Snakes and Ladders or Snap, or even hear the dinner lady tell them to join the back of the queue. For these children, when faced with the roll of the dice, there are three possible courses of action. They can avoid playing; they can, when they see loss loom, sabotage; or they can cheat.

Sean, bored of winning an over-played game, or irritated that he might lose it, often resorted to havoc – changing the rules ten minutes in, or simply abandoning it in the middle. Perhaps he felt that cheating and sabotage were easy to justify. In one study participants, when asked for their motivation, responded that it was less about cheating than about evening the score. You see, the cheater is playing a metagame. Everyone else is playing the board, while he or she is playing them. It is why cheating has become the byword for infidelity.

However, like cheating at games, is it easier to be unfaithful in a darkened room? Easier when we drive expensive cars? Or is cheating simply about opportunity? Like being left alone in a room with the Monopoly money, does sleeping with a colleague feel like a chance too good to miss?

I wonder though, for Dad, whether what my mother called 'marrying well' was at the root of it. His sprawling Irish family, all loud, poor and disorderly, did not measure well against nannies and number plates, an imbalance that he was forced to swallow every Sunday over afternoon tea.

Although Dad may have used the excuse that he wasn't having as much sex as he would have liked, maybe his serial unfaithfulness was simply about seeking fairness by unfair means. He was evening the score.

Lie ii: We've posted you a present

Apart from pathological lying, cruelty to animals is high on the Hare psychopathy checklist. In fact Schopenhauer, who was a big fan of poodles, said: 'A person who harms or kills animals cannot be a good person at all.' Not surprising, then, that it did not cross my mother's mind to think of asking me to foster her orange-and-white cocker spaniel after her death. More suitable adoptive parents were found.

The earliest animal memory I have is of Dad hauling baby bunny rabbits out from beneath the shed and bagging them. He is angry. Two rabbits have become twelve rabbits. He orders Sean to dig beneath the shed, and reaches into the holes that now ravage the lawn. I watch how the bags squirm, and wonder why bags are a good place for rabbits. Sean tells me that the bags are for taking the rabbits to the river. All I can feel is that I am glad I am not a rabbit, but not because they are going to the river. That might be nice. I am glad, because somehow they make Dad furious.

In those days we lived at St Ninian's Terrace in Morningside, Edinburgh, next to a Mr and Mrs Keddie, who, amongst other things, complained about the rabbits. I never remember seeing the Keddies, but we heard them most days, hammering on the party wall, screaming for us to shut up. Sean's footballs, rugby balls, tennis balls, golf balls, all sailed over the Keddie wall, never to be seen again.

Dad had tried scaring Mrs Keddie shitless on a number of occasions, belting her front door with his fists and yelling through the window, but she was made of steelier stuff than anyone else he'd ever met. In the end, our Peugeot packed up for a holiday, the engine running, Dad crammed a very old and smelly kipper through her letterbox. Winning was important.

We would go on to parent animals of every denomination. Budgerigars shrieking from the curtain rail, goldfish won at the fair, many dogs, a cat, rabbits, mice, five bantam hens, and a turkey bought cheap for Christmas. Maybe someone thought that hanging him upside down in the basement would be enough to kill him. He seemed to take days to die.

I wonder if the reason our house was filled with fur and feather was because one of us was an animal lover, but I hesitate to imagine who that might have been. Deaths were not marked by flowers and songs in the garden or by planting a new tree. Instead there would be an announcement over breakfast – one more animal was a goner.

The afternoon we lost the mouse, I was an accessory, leaning against the side of the bath, the edge of it denting my chest. Sean had the tap on and the plug in. The water thundered out of the faucet, two plastic boats rolling in its wake. There had been floods before, but not that day, only because Sean did not want me to be able to touch his boats. They bobbed out of reach. One had a paddle wheel, and Sean wanted to see if, like the neighbour's hamster, the mouse would make the wheel turn.

A year later two budgerigars were found flat on their backs one morning. They had, in their hunger, eaten the tomato plants. Fairground goldfish, appreciated for their limited life expectancies, were often, if they made it beyond a week, recklessly flushed down toilets where they had been put for safekeeping during a clean.

Throughout this period Trudy, our white miniature poodle, remained understandably nervous. Being in her presence was like looking in the mirror. Morning and evening she was taken out into the garden and yelled at by Dad to 'BE QUICK'. Promptly, without fail, she was. Until, with age, she became not quite quick enough. Inevitably there were accidents on the new lino, and these embarrassments were fatally hard to forgive.

Dad, you see, was a dab hand at potty training, claiming he'd done me in a weekend. A success that perhaps he should not have crowed over in my hearing; I had seen him train the dogs. If they made the mistake of committing to a hesitant piss in a far corner, he dragged them by the scruff, walloping them all the way through to the garden. All the dogs, bar the last – that much-loved orange-and-white cocker spaniel – lived in fear. Their eyes were glazed with it.

On the whole I would have put the unseemly number of deaths and any attendant zoological panic down to inexperienced parenting, if it weren't for Cindy.

Cindy was a tabby, a stray, all heat and loyalty. We took her, or more reasonably stole her, from St Ninian's Terrace when we moved. Mum and Dad locked her into the derelict interior of the new house with only butter on her paws for sustenance. There were mice. She lived there alone for the six months it took to renovate, only to be disappeared a year later, in the autumn of 1977.

Mum thoroughly disliked cats. Her nose wrinkled at the sight of them. When I asked her what had happened to Cindy she said: 'She went to stay on your uncle's farm. She joined a whole load of other cats on the farm.' What's dubious here is the repetition.

Lie 12: We don't have favourites

It is the summer of 1974 and we are camping in Brittany. The caravan has been dragged all the way from Edinburgh and plonked behind the grassy dunes. Every night we play cards – *bouchon* – with a painter and his wife. The game requires quantities of bottles of wine to be drunk first, so as to provide corks.

It must be evening, the adults already a bottle or two in, because the sun is low in the west, the wind blowing horizontal, the way it does in Brittany. The beach, which is never very full, is now deserted, and we are digging a hole. Ed, ignored all day, has in his desperation to be out of Coventry agreed to Sean's suggestion that he be buried up to his neck. The tide creeps towards us as we dig. Adrian decides that we'll do him standing up – Ed is small enough to make it only a little more work, and, he and Sean agree, it will make it much harder to escape.

Ed climbs in, his grave nice and deep. Sean, pleased by Adrian's attention, compacts the sand hard. Ed flinches beneath his hands, the sand splitting the way it does when a body moves beneath it, great cracks opening up. Sean and Adrian bait him to keep still.

Soon he is crying, and I am running over the dune, my bare feet sliding through the sand. Sean and Adrian are with me. I run because I don't want to be there when Ed is found, the sea circling his neck. Sean and Adrian are running because it is funny. They laugh and shout at our little brother from the safety of the dunes, the tide flooding in. They tell him we are leaving him.

He will drown.

I look back from deep within the mahair grass and I see Ed's wee head, camouflaged, his red hair melding with the sand, and I hear the terrible sound of his terror.

Lie 13: I'm the most hard-done-by

What right does anyone have to rewrite their sibling's story? This is not the tale my brothers would tell of themselves.

Nothing in these pages will match the memories they hold. Our age, size, mood and personality will have dictated how we filed these events, and always there will be much to contest: for instance who was most hard-done-by and who remembers it best? All of us build the sort of memory that is most comfortable to live with. It is not what happens to us, says the psychologist Dorothy Rowe, but how we interpret it.

Our brains create the world for us inside our heads. I literally see things differently from the way my brothers do. A Berlin optician was appalled to discover I held a driving licence. I have amblyopia, or lazy eye. My brain compensates for the misalignment in my eyes by ignoring half the visual input, making depth difficult to calculate. I cannot park.

I also experience life differently. Our birth order, our gender, our genetic inheritance mean that the way we see our 'growing up' is unique. This means siblings often have disputed memories. The drowning of the mouse by paddle boat is one example. Maybe Ed was witness, or Adrian, or no one

at all. I can only pretend I remember, because Sean recounted the story numerous times. I'd have to concede that watching a mouse's long struggle to live is not in my memory, and it should be, because death is always going to be hard to watch.

One recent study on how well people remembered their socioeconomic status as children found that 53 per cent of sibling pairs did not agree about the extent of their father's education and 21 per cent disagreed over how much their mother had worked.

When I asked my brothers if Mum ever had paid work, Adrian, because we're not speaking, could not be included in my sample, but Sean responded by text: 'Yes Mum was a sectary [*sic*] some thing like that x'. Ed listed secretarial work too amongst a list of voluntary positions – children's panel, university kindergarten, refugee support. A second email arrived a few hours later. 'She also ran a small private lunatic asylum. Flexible hours.'

It is probably better then to look at things in terms of intention. Philosophers draw a line between truth and truthfulness. Truthfulness is an intention to be honest and truthfulness is my intention between these pages. Fessing up over the mouse is a naïve tactic. I hope you will trust me more. Naïve, because obviously any suggestion that puts my rememberings in doubt could pollute them all.

Yet we all misremember, and most often our intention is not dishonesty but a self-serving desire to feel more comfortable with who we are. In studies of ten memories which involved disputed 'achievement' amongst twins, every individual claimed first place in the sprint, or the spelling prize as their own. The other popular site of argument is victimhood. In the same study only 10 per cent allowed their twin to claim misfortune. We pretend to ourselves that we are the child who was beaten up by older boys, rather than the child who fled. And it is victimhood where we Doyles find the most disagreement.

Much more important than whether I've lied about being in a bathroom when a mouse died will be if I've fully recognised the extent of my elder brothers' experiences. I should. In our earliest years we spend more time in the company of our siblings than anyone else. With our brothers and sisters we form anxious attachments, hoping they will love us, fearing that they won't. What we fear, Rowe suggests, is 'annihilation'. And those best equipped to annihilate us (intimate as they are with our weaknesses) are our siblings.

Yet if I ever had heroes then Adrian and Sean were mine. I wanted them to love me. But how could they? Life had not been fair. Ed and I were proof. Dad used to say Adrian bore the rest of us resentment because he was 'spoilt'. I imagine it was less to do with being spoilt than with finding his nest invaded by a Sean-shaped Tigger. This invasion, one sibling by another, can feel like a loss of identity. Rowe tells us that although the ignominy of being unseated may with time diminish, it will never disappear. This trauma was followed a year later by the death of Adrian's mother.

From Dad's own jealous account Adrian's mother loved him so completely, it was as if there could be nobody else. 'Spoilt' doesn't begin to cover the loss he must have felt.

We never escape the idea of ourselves that our family tells. To nail my siblings to the page like this may feel to them like aggression. They would probably find the account I have given unrecognisable. How would they paint me? Adrian's final correspondence called me a bully (over an incident you'll hear about later). To Ed I am sometimes hostile, and too preoccupied with the past, while in Sean's eyes I will always be Miss Piggy. He does a great impersonation of her angry squeal.

'I've been reading this book, Mir,' he said to me recently, 'and it could change your life. Really change it. Because anger isn't healthy.'

Lie 14: I'm your only girl

A year after Brittany it is me who is in Coventry. I stand on the road, the wrong side of the fence, exactly as Sean has told me, hoping that soon Ed will be dumped in favour of me.

It is summer, and every week the three of us have ranged over the fields and fences, Sean in charge. The tree Ed and Sean are climbing is huge above me, its branches spreading out over the road. Every time a car drives past the leaves graze the roof. I can't see over the wall into the field, and the wooden gate is as high as my forehead. I give up. The verge is steep and grassy and I sit down, listening to the sound of my brothers in the tree above me, Ed being ordered about. There are dandelions and daisies, and the grass has not been cut all summer. It is long and lush. Across the road from the tree is the Hopetoun estate gatehouse cottage, and a cattle grid. A car grumbles across it, disappearing towards the main house. Then everything is still.

Until Sean screams:

'Mir! MIR! RUN!'

He is already out of the tree and over the fence, his hand reaching for mine. We are running, Sean hauling me towards the gatehouse, I tripping and dropping through the cattle grid, as he shouts and shouts and shouts. I think it is part of the game. But then he is hammering on the cottage door. Hammering like someone might die.

Only when it opens and we fall inside do I hear the angry buzz. Five wasps have managed to get into the house with us, and a woman in her pinny is folding a newspaper into a truncheon as more escape out of Sean's shirt. He tears at his clothes.

'My little brother's still in the field,' he tells her. 'He's too small for the gate.'

It's an age before we hear Ed's howl. Finally he's in the

tiny front room with us, in a ball at my feet, the woman beating him with her newspaper, on and on and on, as if she would kill him if she could.

Maybe that is why my parents do it. To make up for the wasps. Because a fortnight later, once Ed is back home, he is given a First-Ever-Brand-New-Bike the day after my birthday, and the day after I have been given my First-Ever-Brand-New-Bike too.

As soon as I see his red Chopper with wide white tyres I tear up the stairs to the bathroom and lock myself in. Dad follows, pounding on the door.

'Ed's your favourite!' I shout. 'It's not even his birthday.'

'But Mir,' he lowers his voice in case the rest of the house might hear, 'you must know that you are my most favourite little girl.'

I kick the wall.

'I'm your only girl.'

Lie 15: One day I'll run off and join the circus

I wish I could remember him for you, but it's as though my brain has made a unilateral decision to trash what it cannot trust. Like sour milk Dad has been discarded.

He liked milk. In fact he liked all plain food – boiled potatoes, scones and jam, a decent sponge, pork chops, lamb not ruined by any bogus herbs. He hated cooked tomatoes and he hated cooked cheese, but adored a sweet trolley

43

where he could see a selection and be able to choose. He also loved freebies, so if it was a buffet he organised his food across the plate in terms of density and shape, so that it could be efficiently stacked and filled. On flights, before Ryanair ruined everything, he left the plane with blankets, pillows, headphones, in-flight magazine, toothbrushes, and any uneaten food. If the chair hadn't been bolted down he would probably have lifted that too.

To settle himself he wrote, working things through on the page. In that difficult period between the priest's edict about marital contraception and Sean's adoption, he wrote fantasies about escape and other women. All handwritten in faded orange jotters; in one he negotiates with his wife the use of a 'prophylactic' (without success), and in another a young woman he meets on a bus carries one in her bag.

Although he discussed with me a Mills & Boon creative writing class, and ideas for a Cold War thriller, neither of these plans for a novel were committed to paper. Perhaps on the page he could not bear to be anything other than himself. Only there could he escape the make-believe that he forced himself to live by.

The judgement of others mattered to him, and therefore by the sheer force of his character it must have mattered massively to me. Perhaps of all his children he needed me to believe that he was a different kind of man. It was me whom he sought out in the gaps between other liaisons. The one woman he hadn't had sex with, or hadn't speculated on conquering. His fiction was important to us both.

Dad came from an island on Ireland's west coast; his

Heimat was the beach. Any beach. He'd stride along the breakwater, his wetsuit peeled down so low you could see the seam of his Union Jack Speedos and often the less sightly seam of his bum.

The sixth child of eight, his head had been too big at birth, and with it wedged and crowning the other islanders tipped his mother into a rowing boat and sent her ashore. Perhaps this sense of being trapped was a formative experience. He was always trying to escape something. His marriage. His life. I bought him a T-shirt the Christmas of '89 which read: 'One day I'll run off and join the circus', which he wore off and on for the rest of his life.

Photographs of him show a man salted and brown, smiling, eyes creased and handsome, a Laser dinghy behind

him, the windsurfer board propped within reach.

Mum, on the other hand, is always at some distance, often amongst a crowd. She's only in the shot because she was caught there, and though she always talked of herself as overweight, in these images she's a woman of average build, with stocky legs, in forgettable clothes.

She and I would watch him stalk and preen across the sand, giggling. It was the only light relief we'd get all day, cowering like mole rats in pockets of shade on whichever beach he'd dumped us. I suppose my mother laughed at his conceit to make herself feel better. But for me it was a desire to taste humanity. The soft bit of him. Something on which I might chew.

Right up until the end he liked to rescue others: a couple refused respite care for their autistic adult son; the female Pakistani lecturer bullied at work; the youth club threatened with a loss of funds. Always he argued the case for those less bellicose than himself. To many he was a hero. He loathed disparity and unfairness, and thumped MPs' desks week after week till something was done, wrote letters tirelessly on others' behalf. He was a mentor and a believer, having courage where others had long since fallen into silence and despair.

Towards the end of his life he became obsessed with senior management corruption at the university where he worked. Evidence of a senior staff member's foreign holiday trips, his nepotism, his dubious bonuses and his decision to charge the university for garaging his car at home was all documented by hand, and all endlessly discussed.

When the felled principal retired prematurely, Dad stacked his files of evidence in the loft and took retirement himself. His final years were paced away along a stretch of Scottish west coast, awash with flotsam and weed, the dog cantering ahead of him, the wind hard against his face.

Down at the shore, his footprints swept clean by the sea, perhaps he struggled with his lies. The rescuing all done, there was no longer anything to distract him from the fact that what he'd never been able to do was escape himself.

Lie 16: Ma's gone to get the messages

In a phone call a family friend tells me that it was only after Dad died that Mum realised how indecent his haste had been in replacing his first wife.

'Your mother must have found the death certificate,' says the friend, 'and realised that the poor woman had only been in the grave a few months.' She hesitates. 'Maureen didn't really know what he was about.'

'What do you mean?'

'Back at the start. She didn't know what he was about the night we met him.' There is a pause on the line. 'I always thought there was something untrustworthy about him. He was just too smooth. Of course a very attractive man, with a good job, but . . .' Another pause. 'I'm sure he was fond of Maureen. But really what he was after was a mother for those children, and any one of us there that night would have done.' I press my forehead to the plaster wall, wanting the cool of it. 'Being a widower, there'd have been the threat of those boys going into care.'

Dad came from a family fearful of social workers. You have to have suffered a certain social deprivation and poverty to develop the kind of fear he and all his siblings felt for children's homes and care. One-way tickets to Australia and institutionalised abuse were truths this family already knew, and they'd been run out of Ireland trying to escape them. Too many handouts at the foodbank, too many busybodies with an opinion on single parents, and too many feral children: all became reasons for the authorities to intervene.

'I developed an attitude to social workers back then,' Dad's brother told me, 'that I've held all my life – Save a Child: Kill a Social Worker. I could smell them from miles off. If they came to the house to see what was going on, I'd not tell them my mammy was working. I'd shout through the door: "She's gone to get the messages."'

But even if we try to forgive Dad his indecent haste, this lie was much harder for my mother to live with than any of the others. He had pretended his wife had been dead much longer than the unseemly few months that she was. This first untruth of their relationship, voiced within hours of being introduced, she never spoke of. Perhaps because she felt it was his worst. Or because I was an entirely unsuitable confidante.

Once I'd left home, each time one of Dad's weekend trips came up for negotiation, or a complaint erupted over how much time he was spending with a colleague, I was primed to take his defence:

'That's ridiculous. Come on, what is it exactly that you suspect him of doing?'

One entry in my diary from as late as 1995 noted that 'Mum and Dad have had another set to.' Apparently five house guests were kneeling on his carpet. 'Praying for me,' he said when he rang.

'No wonder he's furious,' I told her.

But when I bullied her like this she would never answer, swallowing all she might have said.

It was not until eighteen months after his death that she finally broke cover. What provoked her I will never know, because the sexually transmitted disease announcement didn't come until months later. Was it the dreadful Norfolk campsite we were attempting to holiday on? The rain? Or was it just my irksome credulity? My smug and ignorant tone?

I often think it must have been the latter. She'd plainly run out of patience. Driven off the ugly beach by another squall, she announced:

'Your father had an affair with that German tour guide in Cyprus. I found a letter in his stamp collection. He must have kept it for the Italian stamp.'

Reaching the caravan door she knocked the sand from her shoes.

'You know, I had this strange dream last night. I was holding your father's neck over the kitchen sink, wringing it like a chicken.'

Lie 17: *I've lost my mother*

Guilt has the smell, the taste and the look of love, but is nothing like it. There was the guilt that I was not good enough for my mother, and for my mother's part, the guilt that she didn't feel about me the way she wanted to.

I ring one of her friends, casting round, wanting others to tell me what it is I should remember and how I should feel. The first says: 'Maureen was troubled.' She means troubled by Dad. The second says simply: 'I wonder if we ever even knew her.'

Everyone though, when I ask, mentions God. To me religion is like Iraqi WMD. A justification. A fiction. People throw in their lot with God because he confirms beliefs they already hold. For Mum there was also a bonus. Jesus was redress. Jesus trumped everything. And everyone. Dad could not compete. Cuckolded by Christianity, he was probably the first to realise that her infidelity with Christ was more brazen and more enthralling than any of his own affairs. She told me grimly, when I found her crying in bed one afternoon, that Jesus was the only man she could trust.

Rattling my thoughts for the shapes and sounds of her, I'm embarrassed to say I remember the irritation first. Standing beside her in churches and chapels, wishing I were anywhere else. Besides the fact that there would be a sermon to be got through, there was an intensity to her singing that put my teeth on edge.

Yet singing was what she loved most about worship. She would get to her feet to belt out a familiar hymn, her hands raised over her head. Christianity enabled her to help others. Every week she drove all the way over to Lanarkshire and the Dungavel Detention Centre, with toys and food for the imprisoned children, offering practical support with asylum applications, contacting lawyers, sponsoring families so they could be temporarily released, sometimes to be at home with her.

Many people loved her. Yet we both found love so hard. She told me that in one session with a therapist, when asked to arrange her family with chess pieces, she had huddled herself alongside everyone else. Then parked me way off, she said, gesturing with her hand to the corner of the table:

'Right over there.'

As a child my mother had not been easy to love, and what follows remorselessly from that fact is that neither was I. With violent red hair and an Elastoplasted left eye (so as to force the laziness out of my right), I was not the most attractive child. Later she would coerce me into attending Jane Fonda exercise classes and going on a diet. Later still there were the poor examination results, and my poorer choice of men. Perhaps it was easier to have these dissatisfied feelings for me, rather than for my elder brothers. Ambivalence towards them she never allowed herself to voice. Escaping those phantom babies must have been difficult too, the first one who was terminated, and the second who died. Not able to take up thumb-sucking or smoking themselves, they weren't able to disappoint.

Don't we all want our mothers to love us? Harry Harlow, a primate researcher in the seventies, proved that we are programmed to attach, without judgement, to whoever parents us first. Harlow removed rhesus monkey babies from their mothers at six hours old and gave them over to inanimate substitutes. What he found was that, more than milk, these monkeys, mothered by terry cloth, bottle and wire, wanted their unfriendly surrogates very, very much.

Dubbed the 'motherless monkeys' they were as mother-less as Mum, mothered herself by little more than cloth and bottle and wire. The unmothered do not, when they come to parent, in Harlow's view make for 'competent carers'. They trail their unlove with them.

One afternoon I traipsed after her through John Lewis, moaning about the many things a fifteen-year-old has to moan about. In an attempt to hide my weight I was wearing ugly, oversized clothes, a ragged overcoat bought in Oxfam and a pair of DMs, my eyes ringed with blunt black eyeliner.

I lost sight of her on the ground floor, arsing about at the perfume counter. I began to zigzag between the racks and shelves, through handbags and stationery, my pace picking up as the minutes began to drag. Where was she?

I glanced out into the main shopping mall, and up at the chuntering escalators, wondering what happened when teenagers lost their mothers. Long past the stage of being able to utilise the shop tannoy I trailed on and on in a state of faux indifference. Fifteen minutes later I found her, tripping over her bag as I systematically worked the card section. She was slumped on the floor hiding amongst *New Baby* and *Get Well Soon*, tearful:

'I saw two friends I'd have liked to have stopped and talked to, but I couldn't, because YOU were with me.'

Lie 18: The man will come with big scissors and cut off your thumb

Sean ruined primary-school Christmases telling everyone the truth about Santa. A boy called Peter ruined ours. Like most people I lied to my children about the man in a red suit who brings gifts. I also claimed that fairies need teeth.

Once our children find us out on both these counts, there's often an unwillingness to discuss it. We put this down to the younger generation's mercenary calculation that if they let on, the presents will dry up. More honestly, the reason neither side raises the subject of Father Christmas is that parents know they have been a disappointment and children know it too. The more investment both sides have made in the lie, the more difficult it is articulating why, even when it comes to Santa, a lie can feel like betrayal. Rather than talk about it many of us will play out the pretence for years with the stocking and its tangerine, because all of us wish that the magic were true.

The reason children are more gullible with their parents is because they want to believe those whom they love. They make assumptions. The least they expect is that their parents will tell them the truth. When we lie to them, they are put in the difficult position of having to choose between trusting themselves and trusting us.

To trust is also simpler. The lying landscape is confused. Children are told that lying is a crime. Sometimes they are beaten for it. Yet within hours and days they will hear a parent doing it, or even in some cases find themselves being asked to lie on that parent's behalf.

We coax those in our care to keep secrets – the visit with a part-time parent where Roger fell into the pond, or Edith was taken to A&E, a pea lodged up her nose, force a child to collude with one adult, while alienating them from the other. These lies are provoked by self-interest. It is a behaviour children recognise from the playground, where truth privileges the few.

The lies that parents tell can be coercive. Some of us, facing another meal without any eaten vegetables, have resorted to the word 'police'. Psychologists, when speaking of these lies, use the term 'instrumental' as if there were something innocent in telling a child that you will kick them out at the next service station, or if they don't quit sucking their thumb the nasty Struwwelpeter man with big scissors will come chop it off.

Parenting is a not a job that comes naturally. Often we take the easiest option, following blindly the example of those who have gone before. If deceit has been a tool used against us, under pressure we tend to fall into bad habits and use that self-same tool ourselves. There's nothing like facing the gummy innocence of a primary-schooler asking: 'How come Jane's daddy was crying at school?' or 'Why did Auntie Barb fall over?' to force those of us who should know better into making it up on the spot. The whole truth – like Jane's mummy is having an affair with that smarmy father in year five, or falling over is what happens when Auntie Barb has had too much to drink – just doesn't seem appropriate. Why wreck innocence? It is this *whole truth* many argue

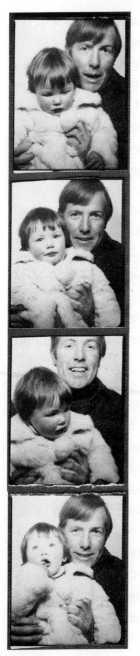

that we are guarding against, because the truth is more information than anyone under sixteen needs.

Infidelity is one of those crimes that come under the *whole truth* umbrella. Fifty-seven per cent of men and 54 per cent of women admit to committing infidelity at some point in their lives. I have done it. Perhaps you have done it. It is a betrayal between two adults, and is unseemly detail that children, we tell ourselves, would not understand. Nor is it anything, we say, that affects them directly. Infidelity is just a symptom of more substantial problems, and under these circumstances we tend to withhold.

Withholding is a parental favourite. However, like a great novel, where plot is lovingly revealed through behaviour, silence is often partial. The clues are all around: finding one adult on the sofa every morning, and the other furtively going through the texts on the other's phone, tells a story that seethes with questions which children are too afraid to ask.

Silence often makes a subject impossible to broach. It is lying without us having to face the fact that we have done so and is a form of deceit sanctioned by the Catholic Church. The doctrine of Mental Reservation stems from St Augustine's belief that hiding the truth does not qualify as deception. Mental Reservation is a way to fulfil an obligation both to be 'truthful' and to keep a secret that is Catholicism at its worst. For instance, although senior clergy in Ireland said they had co-operated with police who were investigating allegations of crimes against children, they omitted the word 'fully'.

In the case of infidelity the betrayed parent may choose to 'protect' children from the truth because they want to avoid being the bringer of bad news. Better to sacrifice totally to betrayal than risk being labelled the baddie. Poor Mum.

Though the Protestant God she prayed to did not have the flexibility of his rival, who allows absolution to be dished out by the priest, she shared a bed with a man who was well versed in the Augustinian principles. Dad understood that as long as a Catholic can stay alive for the time it takes a priest to administer the Last Rites, heaven awaits. In fact he was so motivated to have this final forgiveness that on Monday evenings he trained up my mother's Episcopalian minister to perform it when the time came. The Last Rites are like declaring yourself bankrupt without losing the house or the car.

But perhaps I am looking at all this the wrong way round. In the end Dad could not trust his children to allow him to be his true self. Particularly me. He colluded, hoping to protect me from my own disappointment. He understood that what I wanted, like the man in a red suit with presents, was the father that he was not.

Lie 19: The Da was taken

The week of his twenty-eighth birthday Dad learned in a single telephone call that his father, Michael Doyle, was both still alive and recently expired. It was 1962. Though Michael had been dead to his family since 1938, it took him another twenty-four years to finally pass away, choking to death on the morning of 14 December in Antrim County Lunatic Asylum.

Dad was the son of a lighthouse keeper. The story went that Michael Doyle fell ill on the Maidens Lighthouse, a

treacherous offshore rock in Ireland's North Channel. Dad was not quite four. His mother, Rose, spoke of a storm and of delays. Many days passed before the weather made it possible to reach him.

When Rose spoke of her husband's disappearance, she would insinuate that he was dead by using the phrase 'When the Da was taken'.

'There were always sayings like that in

school,' Dad told me. 'The "taken" always implied being escorted to heaven by angels. I had this picture of him with angels and they're taking him up to heaven, because he was such a good guy.'

By the time Dad received the phone call in Dartford twenty-four years later, the funeral was scheduled for the next morning, three hours' drive from Belfast, on the west coast of Ireland, in Sligo, at Rosses Point.

Death is as important as life to many in Ireland. It would have been disrespectful to let Michael go quietly to his grave. My grandmother must have reasoned that when the time came to bury him, she would brazen it out. In any case 'taken' was not an outright lie.

Dad wrote three versions of his father's burial, working through the shock of being told and the fury it provoked in Pat, his then wife.

'Your mother had no right to let her family grow up and go off marrying and having children without them knowing.'

This and his earlier narratives are handwritten, on loose sheets and in Heriot-Watt examination notebooks stowed in the loft. He writes well. In the first version of the burial, he is diverted from the realisation that his mother has lied to him by chatting up a nurse at the airport. In this story he has given himself more than twenty-four hours' grace in which he can stay at her flat and tell her his story.

In the second version, the protagonist sits through a ghastly supper at his wife's funeral, where despite a generous meal, he feels 'empty'. He is reminded of an earlier grief, the loss of his father, which he describes as being like a swollen balloon scraping the back of his throat.

In a third and much longer rendering, he and his brother wind through the country roads of Ireland, stuck behind herds of sheep and old tractors. They are late. As they empty out of the car at a run their mother appears from within the church. Standing in front of the coffin, she aims her stick at them like a gun. There is a gap on the page, after a half-finished sentence, for about three lines. Then, centred and hanging on their own, perhaps to emphasise the irony, are her words:

He's had his purgatory waiting for you

Amongst Dad's jotters and loose sheets I also found a short flashback from within a longer story. The boy described is twelve, alone in a house, hunting for a pencil and some string. Each drawer of the dresser is 'bung full', its contents wedged in. Frustrated, the boy empties a drawer onto the floor and there he finds the hospital correspondence that certifies his father insane.

'. . . but how inaccessible. Remoter than the grave. I simply stuffed everything back in the drawers and walked.'

The boy walks down to the River Leith and along the bank. There, on the shore, he decides to cut from his life any thought of his father.

'It was easier to accept death than grow up knowing and waiting for a cure. My mother understood that. She had taken the wisest course.'

Perhaps the emotion that he felt for this lie was less rage against his mother than remorse for a boyhood decision. Shamed by his collusion with her deceit, he found himself unable to unravel her lie from his own.

Lie 20: I will not cry

Ed and I are five and seven. In the new house we have our own rooms, and after Saturday night's *Starsky and Hutch*, I sneak through to his. He tells me it's all just ketchup before I climb in beside him. I feel safe here. I am like our cat. She steals up beneath Ed's duvet, or to the bottom of a sleeping bag. She hides.

Adrian has a strange girlfriend with grey skin and straight, straight, straight black hair, and Sean is often in trouble at school. I'm helping him to learn his lines for the Christmas play. But I still cannot tell the time, and Dad has lost his temper about it. He has held me up on his shoulder and shouted at me and the kitchen clock. The panic makes it impossible to work out how long each hand is, or even whether three comes after four, and I certainly don't understand how six can mean both a half and thirty all at once.

I am sorry.

Maybe if we were all a bit better behaved, and I could tell the time, then Dad would stop pressing his lips together and pointing his finger and taking out his belt. Sean gets the belt most days. And if we were all a bit better behaved Mum would stay out of bed.

I find her there when I get home from school, the green floral Laura Ashley curtains closed. She tells me that sleeping makes her eyes water, and that she'll get up soon.

Ed is the only person I can trust. He's good at the ketchup line. He doesn't fret his way into sleep, but allows himself to fall. He trusts the dark and beside him, I can trust it too. I only wish that I didn't have to wait till Saturday to use *Starsky* as an excuse.

That year, we'll get an eight-foot Christmas tree, and presents from Father Christmas overflowing down the stairs, and a dinner with six courses. It's as if Dad knows it's all going wrong, and he wants to make it up. Or he realises that when he leaves us, what we remember about him needs to be better than he's been.

But his leaving will come later. For now, Ed and I are counting our money on the floor in Ed's room. Two matching porcelain pigs, heavy with shrapnel. I love my little brother so much I want us to have the same. It is not enough that I badger Mum to let us wear the same outfits. I want us to be the same. To be one. We start to count, lining up our pennies and tuppences on the brown carpet, in piles of ten, and once the floor is covered in copper towers we write down the numbers and find that we have different amounts. I have tuppence more. Maybe I am too stupid to realise that if I give Ed one of my pennies we will have the same, or maybe I'm too stingy, but it is definitely my idea to steal the difference from Sean.

He can smell the lie as soon as he gets home from his rehearsal at school.

'You've been through my drawers.'

We cannot lie for long, and soon confess that we've only taken two pence.

'We can give it back.'

'No. I'm telling Dad.'

'Please. Here. Have it back.'

'No. I'm telling Dad. You've stolen.'

'What's going on?' Dad bellows up the stairs.

'Nothing,' we call.

But it isn't nothing and soon Sean is being beaten downstairs.

Dad has a big leather belt with two tails. I have seen it, but never been bent over for it, and now that we have told a lie and we have stolen we are going to get it too. Ed is already crying as we follow Dad to the Laura Ashley bedroom.

Then I am alone in there with him and bent over. I will not cry, I tell myself, hearing Ed through the door. I will not.

Lie 21: I didn't peek at Barney

Differentiating between lies that are okay and lies that are not takes enormous finesse that some of us never manage. Perhaps this is simply down to developmental arrest, because when we first start to lie, we do not tell any white ones.

From the age of about three most children lie, and once they've got the knack, continue right through primary school. In fact, after eating, walking and talking, lying is the next developmental stage. Until a little person learns to fib they are not quite complete.

Ed wasn't yet at that stage when the linoleum was burned. His weakness wasn't a question of fault, but immaturity. In order to lie we have to make a conscious decision to tell an untruth. It is an elaborate cognitive step. We find ourselves in a situation that offers two possibilities: to do the right thing, or to do the wrong one.

Curiously scientists have found that good bladder control correlates with competent lying. Apparently the 'inhibitory spillover effect', or keeping ourselves on the edge of boiling over, gives us the necessary focus to pull off deceit. Yet I wonder whether it has more to do with learned technique, because when I lied to my father it was always accompanied by a desperate urge to pee.

The neocortex is the newest part of our brain, and makes up 76 per cent of its total volume. The neocortex is that ruffled blanket, the grey matter, which cloaks the rest. Involved in spatial reasoning, conscious thought and language, its size, neuroscientists argue, makes it possible for us to imagine another person's point of view, or as psychologists call it, have theory of mind. It is this ability that is most important when we set out to tell a lie. Developmentally, as children, we need to comprehend first that we are alone with our thoughts; that no one else can know them unless we tell. We also need to understand that there is a truth and that it has an opposite. Then we have to consider our audience. What does it want to hear? Finally we must weigh the balance against possible consequences. What are the benefits and what are the risks?

For Sean there was never any question. When you're beaten so religiously, there is no gain in honesty. It is always worth the gamble. In our house fury had no light and it had no shade. Lying, stealing, wrecking the lino. It did not matter. The reaction was always the same. For us all, Adrian, Sean, Ed, myself, deceit was an essential skill. The only escape we had was simply to get better and better at it. Which we did.

However, lying at any age is hard. Younger children find it difficult to exhibit consistency between the initial lie and any follow-up. It is only by age seven that children are better able to control semantic leakage and stick to their story. For instance, in one study kids who had peeked at a toy dinosaur, Barney, and pretended that they hadn't, responded to the experimenter in ways that reflected their age and ability. When asked: 'What do you think the toy is?' two-year-olds immediately folded with 'Barney.' One five-year-old said 'I didn't peek at it, but it felt purple, so I think it's Barney.' By seven they were pleading a very believable ignorance.

Even from the age of three most children understand that lying is wrong. Yet they lie anyway, perhaps because they observe their parents lying a good deal of the time: 'Sorry,' one might say, 'the traffic was terrible,' when everyone in the back of the car could tell you that it had nothing to do with traffic, but was down to the rushed hunt for last-minute flowers, a wedding anniversary clean forgot.

According to Dorothy Rowe, the psychologist, we tell lies as a way to defend the sense of who we are. Lies give us back the control we believe we have lost. 'The traffic was terrible' will be used by thousands each evening as they try to steal back something for themselves. Yet if the parent has said, 'The traffic was terrible,' to cover for a daughter's lost shoe and the hour it took to find, then six- to eleven-year-olds would judge that kind of liar more trustworthy. A liar who is dishonest in order to benefit others will earn moral approval, while those who merely lie to benefit themselves earn nothing, because even to a six-year-old self-interest is horrid.

Lie 22: All he needs is a firm hand

Sean says 'I love you' a lot, because his many self-help books say it's important. He feels we should speak about love more regularly. When he does I understand that I'm supposed to say the words back, but I struggle. The first thought that pops into my head is: 'But we have no idea what that means.'

At home 'Love' was the bread in the sandwich to 'Dear' in a letter, or it was used to admire Granny's new dress. For many, many years the 'I love you' sentence was extinct. I, at least, feared that lying about love could ruin it for ever.

Maybe then, in this regard, we were honest. Love had no currency. Survival was about as much as we could muster. Except when death crept in.

Once he smelt the darkness Dad felt the need to speak. I don't remember the specific occasion in those last months when he strung those dangerous three words together, but I know from some latent discomfort that he did. I have memories of the grey light glancing in through the ward window of the Southern General Hospital, and my father heaving himself onto his feet. I understood that he was saying the phrase because he felt he ought to, and I only managed to survive the uneasiness of watching him do it because I believed that in his own way he knew love and had loved me, and in the end that was enough.

But for Sean to hear it, spoken in desperation, was painful. They were words that, as far as his relationship with Dad was concerned, he'd stopped believing in long ago. To him the phrase was empty, perhaps uttered only so as to hear an echo back.

Afterwards Sean asked me over and over in a kind of fury:

'Do you think he did?'

'Love you? Of course,' I would say. 'Of course he did.'

But only because that was the right answer. I didn't really know.

Until I came across, amongst Dad's things, a copy of Sean's adoption file. Without a photocopier Dad had written everything down by hand, on lined paper in blue biro. The time it must have taken to copy out these pages, and to contact the Sisters of St Anne for the file, reveals a motivation to record Sean's story for him that feels to me like an act of love.

Sean's mother was twenty when he was born. Her father had received an MBE for his services in wartime France. She spoke fluent French. The person writing the report says she was a 'dear, little girl – very timid' and 'had wanted to keep the baby at first, but is beginning to think it would be terribly hard to do and not in the best interests of the baby'.

When she travelled up to Charing Cross in November 1962 on the 3.20 train she hoped someone would be able to meet her; she was scared to be in London alone and of having to make her way to the hospital by bus.

A few weeks later Sean was born prematurely on Boxing Day in St Teresa's Maternity Hospital, Wimbledon. He weighed only four pounds eleven ounces, and at four weeks old developed 'severe streptococcal septicaemia' from which he made only a 'slow recovery', remaining in hospital until May 1963.

The Meningitis Research Foundation says that meningitis in babies is much more devastating than in older children. Their brains are vulnerable to injury. A newborn with septicaemia is very sick and those babies with a low birth weight statistically are likely to have a 'poor outcome', especially with regard to cognitive function. Sean's adoption notes read: 'it seems probable that the baby's early failure to thrive was a consequence of his infection.'

Sean, if he were a child today, would be diagnosed with something – dyslexia, aphasia – but then, in the late sixties and seventies, he was just lazy. A child who needed a firm hand.

The final correspondence that Dad copied down in longhand from the adoption file is a letter from Sean's mother to the Sisters of St Anne in May 1963. She expresses worry, hoping her baby will be adopted or fostered soon. She thanks the women who have helped her again for their kindnesses, saying that it will be a relief 'to know the baby is in the hands of good, generous people who will love him and give him a better chance in life than I could'.

Lie 23: Being good makes things better

It is summer, though the day is overcast and threatens rain. We are in a Peugeot estate on the A1, crawling over the hills towards the border.

It is just Mum, Ed, me and Sean making this filial trip to our aunt and uncle in the South. Mum's brother has worked hard to consolidate his birthright, whilst the marriage she has made continues to be disheartening. Particularly on this grotty day driving the A1, for she will jettison what most represents the choice she has made.

We have crossed the River Tweed, and watched the hills of Northumberland recede through the back window. When Sean isn't winding us up, Ed and I wave at lorry drivers and count how many wave back. We seek solidarity beyond the car. The boot is spread with cotton sleeping bags emitting a smell of loft and feet and rained-out camping. We move freely between here and the back seat.

Ed and I try to be good. We believe in it, as others might believe in God. Goodness will have its own salvation. We are so good that when we are back in Edinburgh we can be left alone for ages at the fish pond on the ground floor of the National Museum of Scotland. We wait motionless, watching orange colours flit through the water while our mother spends her hour in the gallery upstairs.

Sean hates the way we deceive ourselves. Goodness has never got him anywhere. He is our jester, our tormentor, our confidant, our fool. He is also not quite one of us.

But that doesn't matter. We are equal. Our parents tell us over and over. We are all loved just the same. We know that even though Sean is adopted it makes no difference. The only reason he is beaten so often is because he is bad.

And on this journey, without Dad to scare him into submission, bad is what he is. There are arguments over who gets the window, and games of rock/paper/scissors where he cheats and licks his fingers to flick the inside of our wrists. He has seen the soft underbelly of us both and knows where to poke.

I think that what happens happens at Scotch Corner, but it could have been anywhere north of Peterborough. We are at an elevated service stop, the slip road rising up to meet the petrol station, at an indeterminate time of day. The rain flecks the windscreen, Ed and I still loose in the boot.

When I ask Sean about that afternoon, and I have tried to twice, he slides away into recollections of how he was often beaten till he wet himself. Sean is frustratingly uninterested in sticking to the point. I ask him because I want to work out how old he was, because however many times I do the calculations, I cannot make him any older. Sean was still a child.

'Did she give you a piece of paper to write on?' I ask, because that is the only thing I remember – the hitch-hiker's sign.

'She gave me nothing. No money, no nothing. And I'd done nothing neither. She just told me to get out of the car.'

My parents never deliver empty threats. If they say they

will put us out, they do. And that wet afternoon at Scotch Corner is proof.

Screaming into the rearview mirror, Mum pulls up in the car park and gets out, hauling Sean with her. By now the rain is hammering down. It rolls in fat drips over the windows, making the silhouette of her gesticulations wobble and contort. Sean droops beside her, his hands in his pockets, his shaggy dark hair wet against his face.

My tummy hurts.

When she storms back towards us she wrenches open the rear door, and a chill sweeps through the car. Now it's raining over the edges of the sleeping bags and the family suitcase open at our feet. Soon Mum is tearing into that too, stuffing what is Sean's into a plastic bag. It's only when I clutch my things around me that she seems to notice that we're there. We are ordered to pass her a felt-tip pen. It's a green one, and once she has torn a sheet out from my colouring-in book she begins to write.

The soggy piece of paper is for Sean, for she pushes it into his chest, throwing all the doors closed against him. Back in the driver's seat she fights with the gear stick and the indicator, the windscreen wipers scraping aside a blur of rain.

Her escape from the car park is not as quick as she would have liked, and we accelerate noisily in the wrong gear down the slip road, back onto the A1. As we wave at Sean's shrinking silhouette, his sign still limp at his side, I think he is like Paddington, except the message doesn't say 'please' or 'bear' or 'Darkest Peru'. It says 'EDINBURGH', and instead of a marmalade-filled suitcase Sean is gripping a plastic bag.

Lie 24: One day you'll move into the Big House

My parents' marriage was in special measures by 1977. In an attempt to pretend it wasn't, my mother insisted that we continue our fractious Sunday visits to Perthshire and the Paterson estate. A visit to Granny focused the mind. It reminded my father what it was she had forsaken.

Granny had been sold short herself. She had always believed that once her mother-in-law died, she would finally move into the Big House. That was the plan (and perhaps the only reason my grandmother had agreed to marry). Instead, as soon as her eldest son came of age, he claimed his inheritance, some angry Shetland ponies that strewed the drive thrown in. Granny found herself housed with Granddad in a small modern building in the grounds.

Each window had metal venetian blinds, which must have been extremely 'in' in the early seventies, because every morning and evening there was a great pantomime of hauling the blinds up or down, so the whole house seemed to shriek and clatter at dawn and dusk. Both grandparents slept in separate single beds at either end of the upstairs corridor, a guest room slung in the middle. It too had high single beds that seemed to swallow you whole as soon as you clambered in. Ed and I stayed over often, but Mum only stayed once. It was in the refugee weeks of September and October 1977.

When I blew out the candles on my birthday cake in August I'd made a wish: I wanted to fly. The cake was a chocolate sponge with nine candles and Smarties and I had to stand on a stool to be able to reach. With the cheap pine wobbling beneath me, I plunged the knife in, my eyes tight shut. Perhaps I wanted to fly like a bird, by simply flapping my arms, but I imagine I wasn't capable of that level of ambition. So in retrospect my wish was a waste. Dad had already accepted a job in Saudi Arabia. We would fly.

When Dad took the assistant professorship position he didn't feel under any pressure to tell Mum his plan to leave her. He did, though, feel compelled to deal with what had always held him back. A boarding school was found for Sean and a flat in Edinburgh for Adrian, who had only one more year of school. And once both inconveniences were seen to, he applied for a bachelor visa and bachelor accommodation. Then he bought a one-way ticket to Dhahran.

It was, like all those Irish lies his mother had told him, a lie of omission which left the victim to incorrectly fill in the gaps. My mother, believing that she would emigrate too, was allowed to begin packing, to throw in her job at Edinburgh Dairies, and to worry over whether to cut the Marks & Spencer's labels (a brand then banned in Saudi Arabia) from our clothes. By late August she had rented out the house to a pastor from Hawaii and was fretting over how, on the back of only three suitcases, she would be able to build a new life. Still Dad said nothing. When his own visa arrived in the post the first week of September, he indulged her with a story about Saudi incompetence, and a fortnight later headed for the airport, a single suitcase in his grip.

To have spoken the truth would have freed him. Instead the lie took over. It was a reversal he would perhaps always regret. On the back of some student notes for an Engineering Graphics course he taught, which are headed 'Read carefully, it may affect your grade', Dad has written an 'Epilogue' in pencil, a two-sided postscript to a story that is long lost.

When we find the protagonist, J—, he is browsing through a Sunday supplement and stumbles over an article with the headline 'Family Man Still Missing After One Year'. The wife, M—, when interviewed, tells the reporter she has only been able to imagine that her husband's disappearance is down to a 'loss of memory'. J— reflects: 'If *trying to forget* [Dad's emphasis] equates with *loss of memory* then she's right.'

It is unclear when Dad gave up on his fib. Apart from ticking the 'Single' box in the employment questionnaire, this lie of his was never explicit. More honestly it was an undeclared wish. But to have hoped that Mum would get the hint was never going to be a good plan. It was not until after he died that she realised Saudi Arabia had been primarily about escaping her.

Maybe he chickened out when the Hawaiian pastor arrived to rent the house, allowing us to hang on in our rooms a few more days. Or what broke his courage was seeing how we three, without visas, our lives packed into three tan, synthetic buckled suitcases, had to be rehoused at Granny and Granddad's in Perthshire.

My grandparents were a couple with a routine and a lifestyle that the house struggled to accommodate. There was a hatch between the dining room and the kitchen through which help could be administered. But help had dwindled from a small platoon in the 1930s to a couple of hours of Mrs McGregor on weekdays between the hours of ten and twelve. Abandoned to themselves for breakfast each morning the two of them would scuffle about, pushing and pulling plates and boiled eggs in and out, then retrieve the two types of marmalade (the Golden Shred was hers) and the two tins of oatcakes (he preferred thick) from the sideboard, and they would eat at either end of the table in silence. Apart, that is, from those long weeks in September and October 1977, when, as Granddad smeared his marmalade, he would ask after the visa and the plane tickets, my father's name never passing his lips.

Granddad had a nose for a deserter. Dorothy Jane, Granny, I would later learn, had attempted a similar escape herself.

Granddad wore his suffering about him like clothes. His left side dragging from polio, he hauled one leg along like a dead weight, his lame hand clutched cautiously by his side.

Granny was a woman who felt herself much grander than her life had allowed. Hating to do anything that someone else might do for her, she was the first person I ever knew to buy a then obscenely overpriced Marks & Spencer's sandwich, which she cut down to four quarters and attempted to pass off as her own. She had her hair 'done' twice a week, imprisoned beneath a hooded hairdryer, *Vogue* open in her lap.

Though she struggled to like anyone else, she did like me, with the kind of straightforwardness you can only expect from a grandparent. One letter she sent to me at school reads: 'Please come and spend a couple of nights with me. I find it very lonely.'

That autumn I did my best not to intrude on my grandparents' routines, but our presence was difficult to ignore. It was not a big house, the telephone at the heart of things,

ringing roundly beneath the staircase. The stairwell had a chimney effect, which meant that each conversation could be overheard wherever you were in the house. We all heard the desperation in Mum's voice each time she called the Saudi embassy, and the angry whispers she used the few times she managed to speak to Dad.

One morning after breakfast Ed and I gratefully retreated. Another day yawned ahead of us. Soon Granny would drive into town for her hour at the hairdresser and Mum, minus half her audience, would make that embassy call.

Ed, anticipating the discomfort of having to listen, took off towards the Shetland ponies, or a tree. I tiptoed upstairs, wanting to curl up in bed with *The O'Sullivan Twins at St Clare's* – Erica, the nasty one, had just told on everyone else for having a midnight feast.

On the landing at the top of the stairs I heard the grumble

of Granddad on the telephone extension in his bedroom, speaking to his bookmaker.

Through the door of the spare bedroom I could see out the window the low sun, thin and pale against the trees, the days darkening into autumn. The light through the glass had a dismal quality, the field beyond the garden ploughed and black. It was only then that I noticed Mum's silhouette hunched on the bed.

Despair had stripped my mother from me, revealing a woman strange and alone. I backed quietly into the corridor, keeping my eyes to the window.

Today only the feeling of anxious sadness, and that black field, stick.

Lie 25: They're pestering me to have another baby

The worst lies are those that are planned and well executed. If there was a jail term for the most devious family member, my maternal grandmother would be the one to get life.

I always knew Granddad wasn't who she would have married if she had had any choice in the matter. He was what you ended up with if you managed to fuck up your London season.

From all accounts Granny had had a relationship with her chaperon, who, rather than being old and female as one would expect, was a youthful widower. The other ladies that year made the assumption that she was more interested in him than in any of the young men on offer. She remained on in his Wimbledon home long after the season was over. The more time that passed the more the talk solidified and the more difficult it became to marry.

Only when she had reached her late twenties was a husband found. Mr Paterson, a factory owner from Fife, was new to his money, polio-ridden, and desperate. His last letter in the days before they married, dated 18 July 1938, is fearful of her expectations, positively dreading his wedding night: 'I am perhaps a little nervous now. . . . I don't know what will happen on Saturday night, as I think we will both be rather tired.' He signs off: 'Darling I do love you and I wish it was all over now.'

The questions about the chaperon (seen here giving Dorothy away at the wedding) were raised at about the same

time as Mum began to query her legitimacy. These questions I heard, but did not listen to. I was sixteen and had some extremely trying issues of my own to deal with: could I afford, get into, or even get hold of a pair of Fiorucci jeans before term started?

The questioning of Mum's legitimacy was precipitated by her father's will. He had left her little, confirming feelings she had long known.

Physically there is no question that Dorothy and Ian Paterson's first child, Mum's brother, is his father's spit. A big-lipped, ponderous man with black hair. My mother, however, was a redhead.

Only 1 to 2 per cent of the human population have red hair, because in order to have a red-haired child, both parents need to carry a mutated MC1R gene. The MC1R gene plays an important role in pigmentation. Statistics quoted in *Nature Genetics* reveal that carriers of the mutated gene make up fewer than 20 per cent of people with black or brown hair and less than 4 per cent of those with a good tanning response. Granddad was amongst the 4 per cent.

Though he pre-dated the genetic generation Granddad had resolved that red hair was wrong. He wrote in one letter to my grandmother, in the period before my mother was born, that he would be sorry if his child turned out to 'have red hair', though he bravely stated: 'I don't think it will matter very much.'

He knew, though, that he was being betrayed. Amongst the detritus of Granny's life there is a massive correspondence that dates back to the war.

Reading it, it is possible to see that there can only have

been a brief post-wedding honeymoon period of fidelity before Dorothy fell into bad habits. Soon she was comforting
lonely officers, who were billeted in their house near Stir-
ling. Or more often she was AWOL for weeks and weeks at
a time. My mother remembered her disappearances, regular trips to London, that were marked by how irritable all
the adults concerned were on Granny's return.

Letters from Granddad during this period read: 'I am feeling very sad this morning as there is no letter from you . . .'
or 'I have had no letter from you, only an account rendered
from Graham & Martin for over £460!' (which in today's
money would be a blistering £19,300). Ian also writes that
he has forwarded her engagement ring: 'It was very bad of
you to have left it behind and another time I won't bother
to send it on.'

Other than her chaperon and her husband, the third
correspondent in the letter collection is the fantastically
named Captain Ronnie Rushe. His name is familiar. My
mother had rolled it over her tongue in my hearing, and
after only two letters I want to roll it over my tongue too –
Ronnie Rushe, I keep repeating to myself. Ronnie Rushe
sending stockings from Beirut and Elizabeth Arden lipstick
from Amalfi. A chest surgeon, who published in the *Lancet*
in 1946. This is the kind of aspirational grandparent I want
in my life – the kind of genetic heritage a person dreams of.
I ring up Ed. It's the first time in years he's agreed with me
about anything. He suggests we celebrate with champagne.

Ronnie Rushe is loving: 'I have thought about you very
many times my dear, and have regretted nothing'; 'I never
told [my wife] all – I let her know that we sailed very near

the wind, but always denied anything else.'

Did Ronnie Rushe have red hair, though? I read on, hopeful that something may come up about freckles or burning beneath an African sun (however there is only mention of Rommel). Instead there are hints that Dorothy's marriage is a mess. He writes saying he has sympathy with her domestic situation: 'it can't, I fear be a very cheerful one.' Or asking whether the new nurse is 'safe against Ian's charms'. (Granny often railed against the nannies.)

However, with each letter the mirage of Ronnie Rushe as grandfather begins to dissolve. He mourns the time that has passed since they last met, and perhaps because he is married himself, Dorothy feels comfortable writing to him about her new lovers: 'the American boyfriend sounds rather fun,' Ronnie writes, or 'that escapade with the Naval Officer in Glasgow – you really are the limit. How gratifying not to have lost your cunning.' The name, though, that comes up most frequently is Phil. She wishes to leave her husband and child for him.

In the lead-up to Phil's furlough from the war in Africa, in late July 1943 Dorothy raises with Ronnie (and probably every other person she is speaking to) the question of another baby. She claims that her in-laws are 'pestering' her to expand the family. Then she reinstates Ian's 'fortnightly visitations' and tells everyone in her circle of this decision too. The resulting gossip makes sexual intercourse with Phil possible.

With the time for Phil's leave fast approaching, Ronnie, admitting jealousy, counsels her to stay in her marriage till the end of the war, 'so you will not risk being thrown out or

being penniless'. Then after my mother is conceived, Ronnie, aghast, writes: 'And this time, I don't suppose you have
consulted Dr Maclachlan?' Which suggests there have been
previous illegitimate pregnancies and other decisions made.

Once my mother is born Ronnie writes: 'Ian is behaving
well I am glad to hear,' and 'the fact that none of your in-
laws know of the Phil episode – I do hope you have heard
from him now, after all this time. And that he will see the
force of your decision.' Which was to have the baby, to pretend that it was her husband's and to stay.

It is hard to imagine what my mother took from these
letters, because we all draw from a text only what we need
from it. However, after that brief hiatus in the months following her father's death, Mum dropped the whole illegitimacy project and turned resolutely to God.

Lie 26: I am your father

Illegitimacy. Infidelity. There is much of both in my genes.
Illegitimacy is a catch-all for any person born out of wedlock. It is an outdated definition, reflecting outdated views,
and doesn't acknowledge the silent group of illegitimates.
The ones who are born within wedlock, but not of the father
they think. Here the nature/nurture question is at its most
interesting.

I work for a professor who researches at the interstices between the genetic inheritance from our parents and the environment in which we live. He and his fellow scientists are

preoccupied with that grey area between. How a stressed-out animal and his stressed-out sperm can imprint biological change in the next generation. For example, mice who were not exposed to stress themselves but were fathered by the stressed-out are found to be more likely to underestimate risk, have an upset metabolism and be depressed. (A depressed mouse, in case you're interested, is one that gives up.) A human study has also been conducted by researchers at Mount Sinai University, looking at the children of Holocaust victims. Not only have these offspring inherited their parents' eye colour, musical talent and metabolism, they have, it seems, inherited their stress. Rachel Yehuda and her team analysed the genes of the survivors' offspring and found that there were epigenetic tags on the same part of the stress-related gene in both parent and child. Epigenetic tags choreograph the activity of our genes, and Yehuda and her colleagues assert that these tags can be inherited.

Once a baby is out in the world, the family she finds herself being parented by and the environment she lives in may change the way her genes are expressed, which has an impact on how she grows, and on the children she comes to produce.

So although the sperm that created my mother will have had its own genetic message (a man on furlough from a war) and her lawful father's genes will not, the environment of mistrust and betrayal that she grew up in will also have had its biological impact. On her, and ultimately on me.

Up until the end of the twentieth century sexual infidelity was seen to have a more significant impact on men than on women, because men financially had a lot more to lose.

Like my grandfather, when a partner was unfaithful, the cuckold was forced to live not only with the betrayal, but with the financial burden of another man's child. The research term for this kind of lie is 'misattributed paternity'.

Data on misattributed paternity is most often drawn from men with 'low paternity confidence', who themselves make the decision to take a paternity test. This is a category into which my grandfather may have put himself. Had science been a bit further on in the forties and fifties, we might have found him at the front of the queue.

Genetic origin is important for a person's sense of identity, psychological well-being and personal autonomy. A child's right to know his or her own biological parentage is recognised under Article 7 of the UN Convention on the Rights of the Child, 1989. Lady Warnock, the philosopher who had established anonymity for gamete donors when she chaired a UK parliamentary inquiry on the subject in 1984, later reversed her opinion. On seeing the figures of how many parents of donor children choose to lie, she argued that to keep a child's biological origins a secret is 'evil'. The deception, she said, is of a 'very long-term kind', in which the interests of the parents are given precedence over the interests of the child.

In the case of misattributed paternity the mother finds herself in a toxic bind from which she cannot escape. Even though the proof of her lies has grown inexorably inside her, evidence of her deceit written all over her child's face, it is a secret that must stay secret. A skeleton that needs burying in the darkest places of the psyche, if this is a fib she will be able to pull off. And 'pulling it off' in cases like this is a lifelong endeavour.

Secrets are a burden. We talk of them weighing us down. Psychologists from Columbia and Stanford have found a correlation between the language we use and the way secrets make people physically feel. To be carrying the wrong child must be like having your pockets filled with stones.

Which, with my grandmother, led to an infuriating evasiveness. By the time Mum had found and read the Rushe letters my grandmother teetered on the edges of dementia. Mum and I would sit in her ludicrously expensive room at the nursing home, watching her eyes shift and her words skate as she attempted to manage her deceit. Mum, her bag clasped hard in her lap, would stare straight ahead, like a person at a bus stop. Waiting.

All she would ever know of her biological father was that perhaps his name was Phil. Phil, as a grandparent within me, has been genetically randomised. There will be bits of him, Dorothy Jane, Rose Haran and the mentally frail Michael Doyle littered through me in a mosaic of chromosomes. I am mildly curious about which bits might be Phil's, but to my mother this poverty of knowing became a struggle to know and to understand herself.

Lie 27: The Saudis are all bloody incompetent

In the end, Mum completed the visa application for Saudi Arabia herself.

Ed and I wore matching T-shirts and trousers, outfits she

had bought specially for the trip. As she had once dressed for dinner, now she dressed us for the flight.

Flying, to my intense disappointment, was sitting still, with nothing to look at through the window. British Airways wouldn't be privatised until 1987 and was considered by everyone across the eastern Gulf coast to be the poor man's choice. However the drinks were free, and on the milk run between Heathrow and Dhahran in the late seventies, that was the only important consideration.

In October 1977 everyone on that plane was a worker heading east to the driest country on earth. Getting completely hammered was mandatory, and every adult did. On one return flight into Terminal 3 a few years later, Dad was so drunk the flight crew weren't able to manhandle him into his seat for landing. He flailed about in economy until the plane hit the tarmac, levelling him in the aisle.

But that first evening, as we disembarked, we found the wind blew hot like a hairdryer, and the slow burn of the sun from the sky was replaced by a sudden plunge into night. Far into the distance, beyond the runway, a few orange streetlights marked out a path through the waste of desert, and in the distance huge flames tore into a black sky.

Only in 2006 did Saudi Arabia begin issuing tourist visas, and with huge restrictions – no single women under the age of thirty, no unmarried couples and no Jews. It is not a country that wants to invite the world in. Back then we were mere workers, submitted to a frisk and search, like janitors heading into a jail.

Getting through customs at Dhahran took hours. The long line of westerners were scrutinised bag by bag, shirt by shirt, a mess of belongings accumulating beneath the tables. The queues were chaotic and the inspection team, wearing white gloves, unpredictable. They were looking for ham, alcohol and indecent material. There was talk of women strapping bacon to their stomachs, or smuggling porn in a concealed compartment of their suitcases, but the things we lost beneath the table were more innocent: a children's book, or a jar of olives, making a bottle of gin feel as dangerous as an IED. The Saudi justice system lacked any logic, and once tangled up in it there was a sense that anything could happen. Anything at all.

So, rightly, the Marks & Spencer's clothing was of huge concern as we waited. However, without labels it was impossible to prove our clothes had been stitched by infidels, and so, duly disembowelled, we trailed out from behind the temporary partitions, struggling to carry what we hadn't been able to repack.

The arrivals hall teemed with men wearing identical uniforms of white dresses, their heads bound in red checked scarves, sandals flacking across the marble floor. Occasionally there was a figure swathed in yards of black polyester, hennaed hands holding the material tight over her face.

Of seeing Dad I remember nothing until we were careering through the darkness in a dusty cab, Arabic music belting out the open windows. Looking over into the back seat he told us that there had been a problem with our accommodation.

'We've been allocated a flat in Dammam.'

'Dammam?' Mum leant forward to be heard better. 'You said we'd be given a house.'

I watched the prayer beads swing from the rearview mirror and clutched the back of the passenger seat.

'You wouldn't believe', he said, 'the incompetence of these people.'

Through the windscreen the flames shrank away to the north, the skyline of a town looming ahead.

'Where the hell's Dammam?' Mum asked.

Dammam was where the buildings and roads were unfinished, sand driven up onto the patchy pavements by a chaos of cars. Dammam was where weevils overran our cornflakes and rats the size of Dad's shoe overran the front step. All of it became proof to my mother that he had pretended in his application he was single. The reason there had been no house 'on compound', she said after his death, was because he simply had not applied for one. Dammam, she told me, was where his lies caught him up.

Lie 28: I'm leaving you

Mum leaves us in Saudi Arabia with Dad. There is a threat that this time it's for good.

We are ten and eight. It's a shock. Everything was going so well. Dad had ditched his anger for parties and sailing. Mum had got stuck into the Women's Group. She would make Afternoon Tea each Wednesday afternoon, where scones and tea quickly gave way, on the dot of five, to homemade booze.

There had been time to breathe.

We have a new house too, with grass around it, a stunted palm, air conditioning and a view of the six-foot-high Aramco fence. Beyond stands the baseball pitch and the Rolling Hills Golf Club, its 'greens' held together by tar. Through the wire we watch women in shorts, with squares of carpet, pitch and putt, digging dirt from the holes as they go. They drive huge Chevrolets, living a life that we can only dream of and from which we are roundly excluded. Security at their gates is tight.

The Aramco compound has its own television channel, which we're able to pick up with our aerial, if a wadge of aluminium foil is scrunched around each of its ends. Our world has expanded in magical ways. There is the recreation centre, where we hurl ourselves off the diving board,

and the wasted desert, through which we explore, tinkering in the dirt. Dancing between the sprinklers we roam free for hours.

After Mum goes there are dens built with discarded builders' waste, the scorpion is fed, the camel stroked. Dad is at work most of the time, and in a better mood. We eat a good deal of Tuna Helper, beans, toast in the evening. For lunch we take ourselves to the rec centre for burgers, fries, a slush. The new puppie machine has arrived and the blue ones are best. Perhaps we play a couple of games of pool, go swimming. The weeks are ours and there is lots to do.

One afternoon we come back to find Dad has rearranged the furniture, and the guest toilet has a sign on the door in blue biro which reads 'Men Only'. We are told when we get in that it is absolutely out of bounds. But as the freezer is emptied for ice production, outdoor seating looted from the neighbours, and the bachelor contingent begin to traipse over with plastic cool boxes, we await our opportunity. Dad's mood is buoyant. We take a risk.

The toilet is no bigger than a cubicle, with maroon tiles on the floor and white walls. On the inside of the door, at head height for Ed and anyone seated on the lavatory, there is a picture. A brunette stands in a black basque and panties, one stilettoed foot balanced on a plain wooden chair. Blu-tacked beneath her is another picture. The same woman. Closer. She is now seated, one breast exposed. And beneath is another, and another, a comic-strip undress, the woman's face falling from view as the camera pans down to where it matters; the spread labia, the purply inside of her, raw as a wound.

Hustler's first publication of a woman jacked open was only four years earlier, in 1974. This is on the boundary of unacceptability in the West. And in Saudi it is going too far. The religious police, had they raided, would have lashed my father in the public square.

Later I would remember the 'Men Only' toilet merely as an aberration. A father going crazy in the straightest country on earth. But that night I am too relieved to care. We are on holiday from his rage and his impatience. We live a lie with him, that he is free, and that when the party deteriorates in the small hours to a bedraggled chain of adults staggering off into the desert he won't have to wake up to the truth.

In bed we listen to their shouts fall away in the warm night, disappearing down into the dark corners of the compound, away towards the perimeter fence. They hunt for ages, the women's giggles punctuating each call, and the person we hear them yelling for is George.

I ask Dad in the morning: 'Who is George?'

'George is anybody. Just anybody.'

The man desperate to be free, even from his name. The anybody. The phantom that no one can catch.

Soon after, our holiday from Mum came to an end. We three packed up our bags and took a plane to Corfu. The Mater, as Dad liked to call her, would land a few hours later from Heathrow.

It was a long wait. There was little to do. We bought red roses as a present for her, roses that by the time she walked into the arrivals hall were faded and in pieces, each head loose on its stem.

Lie 29: We're staying together for the children

This habjab, as Dad called Mum's 'I'm leaving you', was not her first, nor her last. She would tell me years later that our empty desert summer happened because Dad had gifted her (astonishingly in an Islamic fundamentalist state) another dose of the clap.

Divorce was on everyone's mind.

There are three legal grounds for divorce: desertion, unreasonable behaviour and adultery, labels that cover everything from poor hygiene to a lack of equality (over 44 per cent of divorces in recent years cited the latter as a contributing factor). The final time Mum left Dad, in the mid-nineties, rather than get to grips with a washing machine he bought in clean clothes from M&S by the week.

Statistics show that there is even a correlation between giving birth to a daughter and calling it a day. In the case of my parents all possible reasons apply, from the most petty to the most ridiculous. So why didn't they?

No courage.

It is the reason people most often give for not leaving their spouse, and from all the evidence Dad lacked courage. Divorce, for any Doyle, is rare. Some of Dad's siblings treat marriage like an extreme sport. Endurance is key. However, I'm not sure that Dad enjoyed unhappiness the way they do. He may have reasoned that hanging around for the good of everyone else balanced out the bad. Staying married may have enabled him to feel less ashamed, and less burdened. In those lonely hours before dawn (he was not a good sleeper) he may have even been able to cast himself as a victim.

But Mum? We find her conflicted, wanting both out and in. And she is conflicted, because whatever it is that the pair of them are up to, perhaps it has something to do with love.

You see, there would be another memorable habjab years later, a morning when we wound up in Girvan. Ordering Ed and me into the back of the car, Mum sat with the engine running, passenger door open till Dad climbed aboard.

She took off at a furious pace, heading south.

Locking everyone into a car in order to leave is not a clear message and it wasn't the first time. She had resorted to kidnap before. There had been an episode in France that frankly is too scary to remember, except as a jigsaw of which only one frail piece remains: Dad's escape. As the Renault rental slowed to hit the bend he forced open the passenger door, then rolled onto the verge, an untidy sprawl, which in memory never gets up.

France Ed remembers. The morning we ended up in Girvan he does not. And he remembers France, he says, because he thought Mum was trying to kill us. We had watched enough television to know – throwing yourself from a moving vehicle could only be about escaping death.

At Girvan there was no escape. Either the coastal road was too dangerous or, having made the mistake of slowing down the last time, Mum kept up her fierce pace. Barricaded in, we were all forced to swallow her decision to leave.

'I want a divorce.'

When Dad refused to engage with her flash announcement she hunted out the two of us in the rearview mirror:

'So?'

I watched the grey shore hurtle past, saying nothing, unable then, as now, to understand what it was we were all doing. A friend has suggested that I hunt for the answer in the lyrics of Randy Newman's 'I Want You to Hurt Like I Do'. We did.

Reaching the seafront car park she threw the car into a space, giving her door the inevitable slam. The morning was grey and thick over the roofs, the cars, the sea. We watched her stomp off to the cafe 'for a coffee'. Dad dragged himself towards shore. I trailed, hands wringing. At the harbour he fell onto a bench, and there beside him I watched as, lost, he heaved dry tears.

Lie 30: I don't remember

Violet and I arrived at prep school, heads shorn, the same September afternoon. It was 1979. Dad was enjoying Saudi Arabia too much to want to leave. Mum was not enjoying it at all, but for the school fees she was prepared to make a sacrifice.

I had been eleven years old for five weeks and four days. Ed was only nine. I counted out the time at school that first term in hours. Violet was older than me by a couple of months, and would have probably preferred to calculate our incarceration in minutes.

She had a tight curl to her hair that required tending with

a large Mason and Pearson brush. When she didn't have it to hand, she flattened the frizz to her skull with a palm. She had pale petal skin and long fingers and this smoothing of her curls, this grief over their loss, became a kind of tic.

Her mother, when she visited, wore Bonnie Cashin. She radiated Knightsbridge and class. My own had the smell of a fading upper class, Mum's confidence thin and off-key. Unlike Violet's mother, who remained silent, mine would spend Sports Day with her hand held out firmly to fellow parents.

'Pleased to meet you. My name's Maureen Doyle.'

To say it was a relief to me that she was only in a position to pay us one annual visit would be a lie. I longed to be with her. Ached.

Violet's parents, on the other hand, took all their visiting allocation. As soon after Saturday morning classes as they were allowed, her parents came to collect her, and I'd watch her disappear down the drive to the best hotel. Violet took pity on me once or twice, and I was invited along for lunch. But when no one took pity, the weekend yawned like a sickness. Saturday afternoons were not so bad. Five hours is not for ever. Mr Hartwell, the science master, devised wild games to distract from the empty afternoon. A blindfold three-legged orienteering race over two miles. Or a complicated search and rescue between boys and girls, which ranged between fields and woods, lasting until dark.

Mr Hartwell was a scary man, with hands that he rubbed together like Uriah Heep. Yet he understood children and he understood play. His classroom squirmed with the hideous and the ghastly, with things that crept and crawled, slithered and slunk. A whole glass cage was given over to

94

meals for the snakes. One large black male rat with his hairless tail transfixed me. Imprisoned beside him within their glass hell was a red-eyed female, the raw curl of herself loose in the sawdust. She gave birth over and over to death, one baby ratling sacrificed at a time.

The snakes were irregular feeders. A corn snake, a milk and a king. The corn was owned by a child who rarely took it out. The other two had been abandoned, mute and unmoving. Sometimes it took them hours to notice the terrified rat, though their homes contained little distraction – a thirty-watt bulb, a stick, the sand.

That first week, Violet and I were turfed out onto the grass to dig for earthworms. It was September, the soil damp beneath the plants that bordered the lawn, rhododendron flowers fading. I dithered. Ed was still the only person I could call a friend. And he was over the other side of the stable yard, bewildered and small, lost to me. I had to find the worm myself and pick it up out of the earth with my own hands.

The boys and girls who had already long been away from home giggled amongst themselves, flicking the first fallen leaves at one another, shrieking over their finds. Thick flesh dangled beige from their fingers.

My new culottes rubbed between my thighs, stiff asylum wear which still smelt of the school outfitters and a mothballed trunk. I crouched, prodding at the ground with a stick. Alone. It was the first time since my parents had gone that the tears hardened round my throat. I poked again, the ground blurring, a stripe of snot thinning along the length of my cardigan sleeve.

In the distance Mr Hartwell took a spade to the ground,

lifting a squirming heap of earthworms into his bucket. When we all trooped back to the classroom, I, wormless, trailed behind. Perhaps Violet is with me here, though I have no memories of anyone but myself. When I ask her she remembers nothing of that afternoon at all.

I find I am as lonely in memory as I was poking the earth beneath a low autumn sun. And it is from this day that I must count Ed, over on the other side of the stable block, as gone from me too. Ever since, his forehead pleats and he yawns when I try to recover this time.

'I don't remember,' he says.

'Really?'

Another yawn. It is the signal that the conversation is closed.

He must remember, I tell myself. He must.

Or maybe it's just that the last person he wants to remember it with is me.

Lie 31: I forgot

To forget is the simplest lie and one that is difficult to challenge. Granny, if asked how much the coat, the shoes or the dress cost, would often claim she had forgotten. It is also the most straightforward way to live with the worst of our pasts. Some of us suffer from what researchers call 'motivated forgetting', an unconscious amnesia that clears our heads of what hurts.

But for most of us, forgetting is a measure of age and infirmity. This morning, for instance, I forgot the words for papier-mâché and took it hard. It leaves me with the scary thought: What else is lost, that I don't yet know?

There are two reasons why we forget. The first is that our brains lack storage. Like Cambridge University Library, which is required to house every word published in the UK and Ireland since 1662, there is just never going to be enough space. Approximately a thousand titles arrive at the library every Thursday in red plastic crates. Piles of books litter most surfaces, snaking spine-up along the floor. There are overflow areas, off-site storage, and platoons of 'fetchers' in the basement hunting down, sometimes on handwritten paper slips, requests from upstairs.

The second hypothesis is poor retrieval, and here we have to imagine the library after a decade of austerity, its workforce shrunk by half. Faced with a mountain of unopened red crates, the library, like our brains, is engulfed by misshelved, poorly referenced material. There is no time for cataloguing and filing. It is an institution gone rogue, operating without any regard for management, or for the truth.

Memory retrieval grows worse over time, not necessarily because of underfunding, but rather because the older we get, the more repetitive our lives become. One commute is indistinguishable from another, so although we may remember this morning's slog on the Northern Line between East Finchley and Embankment, tomorrow only residues of that journey might remain. For the sake of efficiency, our brain will resolve that this information is superfluous. So unless we actively override that decision and consolidate memories, recounting them in the pub or throwing them down in a diary, we are likely to lose them for good.

For liars forgetting is lethal. It is how many of us are found out. It is a serious problem for memoirists too. Not only do we come to the shameful conclusion that we cannot remember vast tracts of the past, but forgetting, at its most brutal, as in the case of Alzheimer's disease, annihilates the self.

Without memory there can be no identity and without identity there is no self. If we cannot remember we have no frame on which to hang the idea of who we are. Clive Wearing, who at the height of his career as a musician suffered a brain infection, is the worst case of amnesia ever recorded. He has told his wife, Deborah, that to live in a perpetual present is 'like being dead'.

Each time she entered the room he would greet her effusively, as if he had waited decades for her to come. In an effort to push back the blankness, or the 'deads', as Deborah referred to them, he kept a journal, in which there are pages and pages of almost identical entries:

'I am awake.'

'2.10 pm This time properly awake.'

'2.14 pm This time finally awake.'

'2.35 pm This time completely awake.'

Clive Wearing's brain, faced again and again with the lie that it had freshly woken, held on to that belief with a daunting conviction, even if it meant ignoring the facts already evidenced down the page.

However, forgetting is not always a catastrophe. To combat Post-Traumatic Stress Disorder, scientists are looking at ways to encourage it. They have discovered that bad memories are epigenetically ingrained; memories of war, abuse and torture literally stain our DNA with chemical markers. One review paper in *Nature* describes how a drug, HDACi, when administered to mice, clears these epigenetic marks. However, it is not known how specific the drug would be in humans. Would HDACi, like a perfectly executed drone strike, take out the single jihadi pedalling like mad through open country, or is the cure a more difficult compromise, where alongside one terrorist a further thousand innocents die?

Forgetting is essential. In fact to survive we must forget. Remembering is balanced and aided by losses that happen without our noticing. Why would we need to remember the name of a work colleague we haven't seen for ten years? Of course when we run into her it's embarrassing, but perhaps we should be relieved that we've not wasted cognitive energy on holding her in our thoughts during the intervening years.

Borges said: 'We live by leaving behind.' His protagonist Funes the Memorious, who after hitting his head is blighted by total recollection, describes his memory as 'a garbage disposal'. A similar view was recently expressed to researchers in California by a woman whose memory is unusually accurate; her recall of past events is 'nonstop, uncontrollable and automatic', and it drives her 'crazy'.

Nietzsche famously pointed out that the existence of forgetting has never been proven. What he means is the strong, irrecoverable forgetting that vanishes the word 'papier-mâché' for ever. Rather like trying to prove there is no monster in Loch Ness, absence is always going to be difficult to demonstrate.

To forget is defined as a failure to remember. There is no word for the kind of forgetting that Nietzsche means, the forgetting which is beyond the reach of remembering. A memory that no longer exists at all. We don't have the language for what theorists call this 'strong forgetting', perhaps, because all of us are sometimes assaulted by rememberings provoked by a snatched melody, or the fragrance of cut grass, a moment we never knew we still owned.

Lie 32: I'm Selina

In November 2013 I sign up for group therapy. It is cheaper. One-to-one is difficult to justify. It's only that I always feel that there is something wrong.

Apart from being cheaper, working in groups reveals the dysfunction of family dynamics. Was it my fault that my parents stayed together? Or maybe there was another reason, because by the time Mum turned thirty-five we had already been put out of the house.

But I do not bring this question to the group. At the first meeting I find half of the others are in a much worse place than me. They are crying, finding it difficult to get out of bed. There is cancer, redundancy, violence, despair. One member says absolutely nothing the first three weeks. Shamefully I wonder how any of it will help me. The other half treat the whole thing like 'a bloody coffee morning', one of the more exasperated members of the group says when everything begins to fall apart in week four.

But before the falling apart I play the game the way everyone else does. A bit of sharing about recent events, some platitudes, a lot of holding back. And then in the fourth week someone asks me about my schooldays and I fall into a silent hole of tears. I am almost insensible, definitely inarticulate, mauling a scarf as though I'm trying to wring the life from it. But quickly my fellow group members slide the discussion back to shore and safety, my surrogate family paddling around in the shallows, as I wallow alone at sea.

Week five the one having trouble getting out of bed leaves. She's just escaped hospital, following a stomach pump at A&E, but somehow the conversation slips away from her, taken ashore by those on their coffee morning, back to somewhere safe.

'I want to leave now,' she shouts.

The therapist holds her back, wanting a better 'finish'. Endings are important.

'Like I need to leave now?' the group member shouts again. 'All I can think about is a bloody cigarette.'

'We didn't listen to her earlier,' I say, 'when she told us

she'd attempted suicide. Wouldn't it be a matter of respect to listen to her now?'

Week six, one person down, the observation is over. I've been looking for a parent and there is none, though it is plain, especially for the person who still hasn't spoken a word, that it is all any of us needs.

Week seven and I'm leading the session. Someone has christened me Selina Scott. I go round the group one member at a time and ask directly how things have been. Follow up on points made the previous meeting, and probe deeper.

I don't want to tell any of them what is going on for me. I have been crying. I cry and cry and cry. When I give up being the parent, I think to myself, who the hell's going to parent me? Boarding-school angst is such a cliché anyway. I hate myself. Maybe that's why I am crying. It's the unspeakable self-hate.

By week eleven, outside the group I am crying more than I am not, and have had to go for decompression in one-to-one sessions at another address.

The therapist asks me:

'This pre-verbal self?'

'What?'

'The incoherent child you become when talking about school?' she says.

I nod, though I find it hard to go along with the idea that I have regressed.

'I wondered what it was like to be the pre-verbal Miranda?' she asks.

I struggle to think how talking about something I don't remember is going to help me at all.

'Chaotic? Maybe?' I say, making it up. 'I always knew that Sean was adopted, and Adrian's mum was dead.' She waits. 'Mothers died and they went away.'

'And fathers?'

Again she waits.

'Dad told Sean, if he wasn't better behaved, he'd be back in the orphanage.'

'And how did you visualise the orphanage?'

'Lots of unhappy children. Lots of beds. Bare walls. Bare floors.'

'Like school then?'

I watch the therapist's tissues, wondering whether before each session she makes sure that at least one frosted white corner is lovingly pulled free of its box.

'Maybe . . .' she begins, but I finish the sentence for her.

'Maybe what I'm realising is that my worst nightmare came true.'

Lie 33: School is really nice

At Aberlour House we were forced to write a letter to our parents first thing on a Monday. After morning run, and our porridge breakfast (Monday, Wednesday and Friday were always porridge), and an assembly, seated cross-legged on the parquet floor, we were sent to our form rooms. That first year it was the science room, my lies watched over by the host of reptiles and rodents, one in-gesting another in glass cages that encircled the room. I found these lies more difficult to construct than any of the others that would follow.

It rained often and I sat in my too-starchy, too-new uniform, watching the tears on the glass. I'm sure I was good at the dreaded grammatical connectives – first; then; after; when. What was impossible was to find the words to fill in those spaces that must go between, each one choked from me one letter at a time. It felt too impossible to write how it really was. Of the few I still have, I read that Ed and I are preoccupied with the weather. We ask what it is like 'over there', knowing that in Saudi it will be blazing sunshine and cloudless skies.

By contrast, many of the letters we receive are almost wholly preoccupied with logistics. Did I receive the cheque? Have Beaver Travel sent the visa? Would I please get in touch with the school secretary regarding hotel arrangements for a transit in Amsterdam? In one letter there are instructions on how to buy a train ticket, and anxiety over how I will travel the ten miles between school and the station to make the purchase. In another they have organised for me, aged thirteen, to be sent a visa application form to complete myself.

A letter of mine asks what date Granny will be taking us out. I'm worried, I write, because I cannot read her handwriting. About that transit in Amsterdam a few years later I worry too. How will we find the hotel, I ask, and will anyone help us to get back to the airport in the morning? What if we miss our flight?

The combination of love and distance in these letters feels like a coach trying to manage a team down a phone which keeps cutting out.

'It was good to hear your voices,' Mum writes, 'and to know that you made it over to Granny's ok as per the instructions . . . . .' (her ellipsis – all five dots – I take to mean that her instructions have not been followed to the letter), or 'Hope the journey back to school went well. The lady sitting beside you looked a right grump.' Dad asks: 'Have you heard from the travel company about your visas yet? You should be sent the passports fairly soon, so look after them – no more leaving them in the wet.' In another Dad says he has spent the day imagining my movements through airports. His plans have unravelled. He is only able to locate me through a family friend. 'You've gone to Kinross,' he tells me. It is not the only occasion the arrangements have not worked out as they should: a lost identity card, lost shoes; a drowned passport and a mounting anxiety that my incompetence will bring all their carefully laid plans to nought.

These letters from home were handed out by a member of staff, shouting out our names as we picked up our orange squash and biscuit at break. Every day, at least once, someone would call out Violet's name. I would focus on the secretary's dog, who drooled copiously, willing 'Doyle' to be called.

After a few years I stopped being interested in my parents' letters. My mother's, which were typed up and photocopied for the generalised recipient, with postscripts sometimes added by hand, were so boring that I often wouldn't bother to read them at all. Even now, only occasionally does something catch my attention and

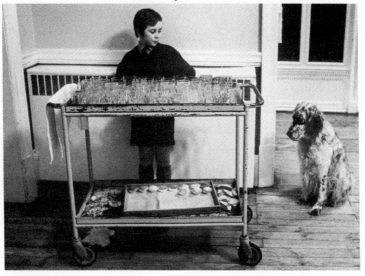

always when the typescript is broken up by pen.

One PS for instance tells me that she's had a sniffy note from Sean, complaining about her typed, standardised correspondence. If I also have a problem with it, she writes – 'Too bad!!'

In my mid- to late adolescence Dad's letters comment on how I haven't written. He underlines how *very* long it has been and that Mum is going *scatty* about it. Perhaps I was no longer interested in spinning the line.

But before, back when we all knew the story needing to be told, Dad says that the best bit of one letter was the last line. According to him, 'I like school and it's really nice.'

Reading these words, I look back to that heroic bent head, my eleven-year-old self struggling to make it up, and can't imagine where she found the reserves for such deceit. Ever since, the bare page has held no fear. I have faced it in more straitened circumstances before.

Lie 34: There will be no morning run

Violet had a green tie dressing gown in soft teddy-bear material, with ghastly appliqué on the chest, and a huge pair of shaggy slippers in a lighter shade of green. Her mother had ordered the entire uniform list, from the two pairs of navy over-pants to six white vests, from Aitken & Niven on George Street in Edinburgh. The dressing gown and slippers were, it turns out, a sales lady's choice.

That first term we were in different dormitories, all named after local castles, or distilleries, it was never clear. In each room there were bare boards, utilitarian bedside lockers with one cupboard and one drawer; the inevitable bunk beds. Each bed was assigned by seniority. We both found ourselves on the bottom bunk.

I was keen. Not to be the best, but to have the whole thing over with. And the thing I was most keen to have over with was morning run.

Morning run was announced by an electric bell hooked up to a switch in the centre of the large Georgian mansion. One ring demanded every child bound out of bed, don skirt (no knickers), cardigan and plimsolls, then run to the front door where a member of staff flushed us out single file. We ran, often very fast, because it was cold, in a large arc around the house.

The bell went at 7 a.m., and morning run began at five past. I was often at the front of the ruffled, pasty-legged queue, Violet blundering in at the back. She had waited with an ever-increasing hope for a second bell.

A second bell, i.e. the sound of one bell immediately followed by another, meant Serious Inclement Weather – sleet, hail, torrential rain. However, some staff liked to leave the gap between two bells so long that I would be in the corridor, already dressed, before the cancellation came.

I never hoped for second bells, and the only reason I didn't was I had forsaken it. Hope brought with it despair, and by week three I had no armour left.

Violet nurtured hope and she nurtured a real annoyance at the unfairness of it all – the terrible food, the morning run, the cold. To struggle against it all was to remain alive.

Soon she was engaged in a Night Raid (always spoken of with its attendant capital letters). A Night Raid was a terrified journey along the upstairs corridor, a journey that transgressed an invisible line separating the girls' side of the house from the boys'. My dormitory was on the way, and beyond lay Mrs Mcleod, the boys' matron. A scary, pissed-off beast of a woman.

That Friday night I was woken by the titters of four

eleven-year-olds tiptoeing through our dormitory. Then came the angry whisper of a senior girl, which provoked a chorus of creaked beds, requests to go to the toilet, moans of 'Shut up!' Then, like the bass line coming into a song, the ancient house groaned a warning. Matron had heard us, and was up.

The light snapped on. Blinking I peered over the lip of my duvet and all I could see, sticking out from beneath Sarah-Louise's bed, like the feet of a corpse, were Violet's huge green slippers. I tried hard not to look at them. To look at them would be to give her away, but I couldn't believe the fact of them. Their hugeness and fluffiness and thereness, all made worse by the fact that instead of standing in the mouth of the door like she usually did, Mrs Mcleod came barrelling through it; a hurdy scary gurdy, screeching in an Aber-

donian accent, her cheap black-rimmed spectacles all fugged up.

I closed my eyes, and when I opened them, she was in the middle of the room, her thick finger jabbing the air.

'If Ah hear another squeak out of yous the lot of you'll be down on report.'

I had never been

on report. Never ever. Violet could often be seen on the black and white marble squares outside the headmaster's office. She knew that the only way out was expulsion, and worked tirelessly towards that fatal goal.

But like a botched overdose, Mrs Mcleod stepped back over the slippers, still with her finger aloft:

'Ah've warned yous. Not ahnother squeak!'

When the door slammed behind her there was silence. A profound silence, eventually punctured by the scrabbling and unravelling of bodies from in and beneath beds.

It's only now that I see that perhaps the lie was Mrs Mcleod's, choosing not to see the slippers. In the moments when she was most herself, asleep in her single-bedded room, she was as lonely as I. Cast adrift from home, institutionalised, hungry, cold, she was an old woman working out her last few years in penury and occasional despair.

But Violet doesn't see it like this at all. Mrs Mcleod, if I were to remember things better, didn't see anything because she couldn't. The truth, Violet would argue, is Mrs Mcleod saw no slippers. They were the indiscernible green mess in a peripheral fug. An obstacle that, like any other, she had just grown good at avoiding.

Lie 35: That woman is ill-disciplined

One of the masters smelt clean, like he scrubbed himself, and wore cords and brogues and navy waistcoats over pressed shirts. Although he was titled he liked us to call him by his initials. It was a pretence at affection for a man who, for me at least, only inspired fear.

To my mother the titled T. was perfect. She was affected by the word of Debrett's – 'the authority on etiquette, taste, and achievement' – and their peerage. She aspired to be a fellow parent to the queen. Sirs and Ladies made for a reassuring start.

My mother often described their first meeting, at which she pointed out that both her children were 'painfully' shy.

His reply would have included an ingratiating smile:

'Don't worry, Mrs Doyle. That won't last long here.'

It was the only ingratiating smile he probably ever gave her. Our school fees were paid by the Saudi government. We didn't even qualify as the new rich. T. preferred the company of the other parents. Before Sports Day, in the summer term, he would have us all on our hands and knees in the flower beds knotting dead daffodils, awaiting the Laird of Eigg Island in his 1927 Rolls-Royce.

Once the shine of Debrett's had worn off my mother minuted (always the efficient secretary), on airmail letter paper, a meeting she had had with him about Ed's worsening behaviour.

'Livid', as she describes him, he had told her that he would get more sense speaking to her husband – 'Aberlour is not an hotel.' When Mum would not be drawn, or would not apologise, T.'s mood worsened. She queried him about another mother and was told that the woman was 'ill-disciplined'. Mum surmised in the footnotes that these words were used on account of the fact that the 'other woman' was black.

On one occasion he introduced a rule that we were not allowed to ask directly for an item in the dining room, but instead had to lure our fellow eaters into offering us what we needed.

'Would you like the salt, Matron?'

'No, thank you, Miranda, but would you?'

The last full day before the Christmas holidays T. announced in assembly that the girls would have a swimming lesson. But because we had already packed our trunks there would be no necessity for us to wear our costumes. They might get wet.

An older girl, Eva, found me fretful in the library. Desperate to get out of it I was too panicked to think of a credible excuse. Eva had no intention of swimming either. Even at eleven the threat of a wet swimming costume seemed to both of us too bogus to be true. It was not the nudity that unnerved me. It was the deceit, because I was never quite as troubled by T.'s birthday baths.

Birthday baths were a ritual. Anyone with a birthday suffered them and on occasional mornings T. came early to the girls' dormitories, before the bell.

With his help we would strip the birthday girl down and drag her screaming to a waiting bath. Whispering about it in the dormitory after lights out, we noted that he preferred to come help with those who were 'bigger'. So Angela's twelfth began in just this way, the dormitory in hysterical pursuit. Two of us took one arm apiece, T.'s huge hands clamped hard to her spread ankles. Swinging her three times, we dunked her in.

Even now this swim, the one which Eva rescued me from,

for some reason seems worse. It is the thinness of his excuse. If wet costumes were an inconvenience, wasn't it obvious that we do something else?

I hunted for the episode in my diaries, forced back to my very first one, which scripts a year at Aberlour House in the most banal terms:

'During activities we had to do the Long Run without stopping. Sarah's tits have grown. Goodnight.'

Unfortunately there is no mention of wet costumes. Neither do I account for Eva's uncharacteristic negotiation with T. on our account. But I do remember that to get us out of the swim she lied. Talk of menstruation would have undoubtedly thrown him off guard – an unexpected gynaecological hiccup that at our age he can't have anticipated. We were released.

Nothing remains in memory of what Eva and I did after that.

I wonder if we watched T.'s knotted fingers, his signet ring catching the light. I speculate on his impatience as he stood by the side of the pool. How countless small hands struggled, as they left the changing room, to cover nipples and the split between downy legs.

But that cannot be the truth, because being a child bystander that morning would never have been allowed. T. would have been the only person at the poolside that morning, and the only person clothed.

Yet I do remember swimming. When I trawl through the tedium of the Holly Hobbie diary I find two occasions that mention naked swims. Maybe because they are optional, my eleven-year-old self does not find the fact of them quite so worrying. On one occasion I tell myself in the diary that I am too shy to go naked: 'We had the birthday party and then we went for a swim. I didn't go nuddy, but everyone else did.' And on another I join in.

The decrepit building where the pool was housed was a reclaimed Nissen hut. It had a chilly changing room, which stank of rot, the blunted light shining through a maxi-glass window.

In memory I cannot remember whether I am wearing my suit, only how we climb up into the above-ground pool, a queue of shy, pale bodies packed tight against the steps. We hurl ourselves at the water, glad of it, the water slopping over the side, slapping time on the concrete. T. orders everyone up against the sides, instructing us to hold hands. He wants a whirlpool. The chatter and shrieks that fill the hut quieten. Together we circle, pulling the water round and round. It sloshes and spills, our faces focused on the sucking hole at our centre, the contents of the pool pouring out.

Lie 36: I have never enjoyed taking a poo

In the two-volume *Encyclopedia of Deception* which I found in the University Library the entry for 'Self-deception' sits conveniently beside 'Self-justification' and 'Self-inflation'. Self-inflation tends to be universal. In a survey of academics 94 per cent placed themselves in the top half of their profession, which can only mean many of them are no good at determining the odds.

Self-justification most of us indulge in too, seeking out people, books and newspaper reports that corroborate our own world view. For instance, I hoover up tales of institutionalised abuse and articles that confirm Blair will always be a megalomaniac, while overlooking anything pro private education or leaving the EU.

The extent of self-deceit is a good measure of a person's capacity to lie. The scientist Robert Trivers makes the case that self-deceit is evolutionarily valuable. When we are blind to ourselves, we are more convincing. Holding self-belief, despite evidence to the contrary, bewitches others. Donald Trump, Donald Rumsfeld, Nigel Farage are good examples. Their conviction is blinding.

Yet self-deception can make us strangers to ourselves.

Did T. believe that he was a good person? Certainly. Did he deceive himself that naked swimming and birthday baths were a positive part of our education? Probably. Did that self-conviction help parents assimilate what was inappropriate? Yes. We lived in the days of Jimmy Savile, Gary Glitter, Rolf Harris: men who believed that groping women and children was part of the job.

The psychologist Joanna Starek describes self-deceit as holding two contradictory beliefs simultaneously. An example might be: 'The kids are absolutely loving school. Loving it.' All the time knowing that their son meticulously packs his bag (and repacks it) throughout the final three days of holiday, while their daughter won't pack at all.

Some might also call this denial. We can deny anything,

even a terminal cancer diagnosis. Denial offers the brain a helpful time lag between hearing the news and processing the consequence. But if we stubbornly continue to deny, it becomes increasingly difficult to haul ourselves round to the truth.

We indulge in this kind of cognitive yoga because admitting to ourselves that we are flawed has its own psychic cost. Believing that we are more generous, more intelligent, more interesting than we are is one way of living with ourselves. We also believe, ironically, that we don't tell as many lies as we do. A little bit of self-deception, some would argue, is normal and should be encouraged. Those who are realistic about their abilities and the way their lives will pan out, say psychologists, tend to be clinically depressed. Depressed people lie less. They admit the horrible things they've done to others and the mistakes they have made. And they are right. Life is not a picnic and sometimes we contribute to making it worse.

Talented self-deceivers, on the other hand, are more successful at school, at work and in love. The definition of a talented self-deceiver is a person who will answer 'no' more often than 'yes' to a list of twenty questions compiled in 1974 by psychologists Ruben Gur and Harold Sackeim. The questions, which were put together during a heavy drinking session in a New York bar, are provocatively shaming. They compel people to deny that they have ever wanted to kill someone else, felt hatred towards their parents, or wondered about their sexual orientation. The list finishes with the most difficult question for many to answer: 'Have you ever wanted to rape, or be raped?' If we answer no, then we are lying, Gur and Sackeim argue, because all of these questions are 'universal truths'. Those of us who fail the test, and pretend that we've never felt sexually inadequate, never believed that our parents were mean to us, are a good deal happier than those who pass.

Joanna Starek, who is both a psychologist and a swimmer, in wanting to understand why one person outperforms another, gave her swim team the twenty questions. She found a correlation between those who failed the test and those who swam fastest. Intrigued, I circulated the same questions to my high-achieving academic colleagues to see whether the results would be the same. Not surprisingly there were some extreme self-deceivers amongst them. Two people wouldn't admit to having sexual fantasies, four never got angry, two hadn't ever enjoyed a bowel movement, and a crazy six had no unpleasant memories. In fact the only one to admit a yes to the sticky question of the rape fantasy was me.

So where does self-deceit leave us with regard to memoir? Truth is extremely important to this genre; it is the fragile wall that holds fiction back. Literary forgery is a crime. To lie about your past, and about who you are, in a book which is marketed as non-fiction, is to piss a lot of people off: ten class actions were filed against James Frey for his memoir, one of the most notorious literary forgeries ever written. The argument is that his intention to lie is what made him culpable, but can we hang a whole literary classification on intent alone?

Memoir will always be a work of self-deception. As an intricate part of the human psyche, being free of self-deceit will be as difficult as clearing dog shit from the tread of a shoe. I have worried over what you will think of me, and whether you'll find me on the page as I want to be seen. These worries have had their inevitable consequences on the truth.

My greatest worry, for instance, is that I might be boring. Some events have been summarily axed as a result. Editing is conscious, but what silent impact has this had on veracity – exaggeration, embroidery, embellishment perhaps? God forbid that you might find me dull.

Concerns about self-deception are not new. St Augustine, who was the first thinker to address the question, 'What is a lie?' and the first to publish an autobiography, *Confessions*, wrote: 'I much fear my secret sins, which Your eyes know, mine do not. For in other kinds of temptations I have some sort of means of examining myself; in this, scarce any.'

Lie 37: I'm going home

Back in the seventies British Airways flights out of Saudi Arabia's east coast departed at one o'clock every morning. Check-in began shortly before midnight. Ed and I would spend the witching hour in one of those seventies airport departure lounges where there was nothing but uncomfortable chairs and the toilet. It was a joyless wait. Through the glass we watched the Dhahran dark, the red lights running away into the desert.

By the time we boarded I was empty, or hungry, I was never sure. But all I remember of those in-flight meals is the sharp orange juice for breakfast. It was as bitter as the five o'clock London morning into which we flew.

During those journeys we were labelled, literally, with red-and-white stripy tickets and a large name badge slung around our necks. The first time, we were picked up before dawn by a 'proxy parent', one already in her senior years. The school sleeper train didn't leave Euston until eight that evening.

Near Leicester Square we ate 'luncheon'. There was white table linen and stodgy food. Ed spoke little, or not at all. I tried my best. Even in the cinema, watching *Moonraker*, I couldn't concentrate for her resentment. It sat square amongst us the entire day.

This arrangement with Universal Aunts was not repeated. A day's entertainment in central London cost the same as a domestic flight north to Aberdeen. Thereafter we were dragged by equally resentful unaccompanied-minor minders the length of Heathrow's warren of underground passageways between Terminals 3 and 1 to meet the first flight of the day north. One letter home from Ed reads that our minders 'just stood there for ten minutes having a granny's conversation about tights!!!!!!'

While he worried that we would miss our flight, I worried we would crash. Following an episode where we had to ditch in Kuwait City after an engine fire, my mother had begun listing in her letters to me some of the world's commercial flight disasters. The PIA incident in Jeddah where all 145 passengers and eleven crew died due to a fire in the cabin, and the Garuda Douglas DC-9 hijacked by Komando Jihad. My letter of 6 October 1980 reads: 'I have

just heard about the Tristar that caught fire near Riyadh, because (it is thought) a passenger was using a gas fire in the aisle. Something like 300 people killed!'

Worry was about all Ed and I did, our teeth clenched most of the way. We had long put our backs to trust, and to adults. One lesson had been clearly driven home. We were on our own.

Arriving in Scotland we'd find that it was still dark, a taxi driver holding up a handwritten A4 sheet which read 'Aberlour House'. Often we were the first to arrive. I would stray between the empty bunk beds upstairs, alone, eyeing the sticky labels on the footboards to see where everyone else was sleeping. On a bottom bunk I would find my Holly Hobbie duvet cover and pillowcase folded on my mattress and like an automaton begin to make up my bed.

As the terms away from home grew, the number of stuffed toys sharing the bed with me grew too. Soon it became difficult to find any place for myself. When I moved on to the secondary school, with regret, I threw these friends away. By the time I was fourteen, while Ed remained in our delegated seats watching the in-flight entertainment, I spent these journeys to and from school at the back of the plane, smoking, getting drinks in with single men I'd befriended in the departure lounge.

I dressed like a homeless person, battered plastic bags in a mess at my fists – wearing an Oxfam overcoat and holed shoes, an inevitable ciggy drooping from my lips. On one flight I 'snogged' a member of the Austrian UN Peacekeeping Force, and on another threatened to bunk with a man I'd found in Amsterdam, and leave Ed 'to it'.

But somehow we would arrive at the customs hall in Dhahran. There, in accordance with sharia law, officials went through every piece of luggage and every women's magazine with gloved hands. They were after evidence of bare skin: shoulders, ankles, necklines, wrists; and, struggling with their own enjoyment, they would blacken the pages with a marker and leave us to repack.

My parents had started asking me in the arrivals hall:

'Have you been smoking?' or 'Is that drink I smell?'

And I'd shake my head, blundering past them with a trolley load of plastic bags, out into the warm night and the car.

Perhaps they would ask Ed too, and he would lie. All we

had left of our relationship was solidarity, and just as I had not abandoned him in Amsterdam, he did not, despite his thorough disapproval, ever tell them how out of control I had become.

The Christmas of 1984 I gave the parental presents much thought. It would be a relief to be able to say that I kept their outrage to myself, so as to save Ed the anxiety. But more likely I had spent much of the journey bragging about how customs-ballbusting my gifts were.

As we approached, the queue snaked long ahead of us, and I'm sure I began to worry too. These flights were often full, and there were many magazines to blight and bags to disembowel, a process I eyed with mounting dread. Once we'd reached the front the customs official held my plastic bag upside down, its vomiting contents falling against the dam of his bent arm.

Amongst the items rolling across the table was a large tub of Johnson's talcum that still shook its powder (though to my immense disappointment, he did not bother to check). Hidden inside the white plastic container was a collection of liqueur chocolates, which Dad eked out till Easter, leaving the Drambuie till last.

Also amongst the haul was a *Playgirl*, camouflaged with wallpaper. It lay unnoticed in my suitcase, along with a decoy copy of *Cosmo* that they so enjoyed blackening out.

The copy of *Playgirl* was a gift for my mother that was as much about wanting to shock her as any Saudi customs official. An early edition, it pictured double-page spreads of penises, laid across hairless thighs. These docile images came to be celebrated as the ultimate insurrection against

Islamic misogyny that any of us women on the compound made. But to me the misogyny was irrelevant. I needed to escape school, and was prepared to risk – alcohol, pornography, sedition – everything to get home. That I never would, or could, has taken me decades to see. Home had long been disbanded, an irrecoverable place in memory to which none of us could return.

Lie 38: I couldn't get him to change his mind

To be honest, if I had not been asked to, I would not write this lie. My memories of it are too thin. You can attribute this entirely to motivated forgetting. The diary entry for that day reads: 'This is the very worst day of my life.'

Yet I have to write it, because without it, Sean says, my lies are incomplete.

It was the summer he returned from the Falklands War.

Dad had missed out on active military service in Cyprus in the fifties, which meant that the only real hero our family had, and has, is Sean. However, though there was a massive welcome at Brize Norton for those returning that August, our hero got off the plane from Ascension Island to find none of us there. A sergeant asked him: 'Hey, don't you have a home to go to?'

Sean felt that he hadn't.

But he turned up anyway, arriving in Edinburgh by train. There the annual holiday pretence at happy families was in its fourth week. Dad had fallen out with Adrian (again) – over decorating the sitting room. Roped in as a replacement, I was being told loudly and often where it was that I was going wrong.

In a letter written years later, Dad blames his diabolical mood that summer on the military. Their poor communication was the only reason he had not been at Brize Norton to welcome Sean home. Then he widens his reach. Apparently Adrian had been 'a bit of a disappointment on a number of fronts'. Therefore he was to blame too. And so was the front room. Dad was decorating, lest we forget. The painting was 'at a stage (one hell of a mess)', he writes, where he could not set it aside.

The decorating sticks with me. It sticks strong in memory, and it sticks strong on the letter page. Why does he bring it up?

His rage sticks with me too. 'Yous yins had to live with my anger,' he writes. So when Sean got home he found us all with our heads down.

Though the BBC had walked us through the whole sorry war on telly, we were ignorant of what Sean's experience had been, the death he had seen, and the broken men he had pieced together. We had watched a sanitised account of Thatcher's war, where there was no mention of bayonets or Tumbledown, and no images that included an army of empty helmets sprawled across the beach. Worse still, we did not think to ask.

Sean did not stay long. He made his escape by bus.

Or as Dad puts it in his letter: 'Sean walked out and I went after him, but couldn't get him to change his mind.'

Which was how it was, in a manner of speaking. Sean walked out and Dad could not persuade him to stay. But there is so much missing.

Sean remembers what is missing. But though I was ordered along to the bus stop I can't.

The shelter, with its stingy plastic bench, was across a busy road, some distance from the house. I'm presuming Dad careered into open traffic. Sean remembers him charging up the street towards him, me in his wake, his fist already up, 'IN A RAGE'. With his finger pointed at me he roared: 'It's Miranda's birthday.'

Recorded in my diary is the 'fuck off' Sean shouted back at him, and the appalling fact that he had to do it 'in front of a queue of other people!'

In that queue, Sean tells me, there was an older woman with a walking stick, and a man who looked too tough to be using a bus – 'hard' is how Sean describes him – and if they had not been there, Sean says, there would have been fists.

'Miranda can have a birthday every year,' Sean told him. 'But you don't go to war every year.'

It was then that the man who was too hard to ride a bus broke in:

'So you've been to war, have you, pal?'

'The Falklands.'

The bus pulled up and opened its door, Dad still shouting, his clenched fist still raised. The woman lifted her stick, other people in the queue gathering up behind her.

Dad yelled that he never, ever wanted to see or to speak to Sean ever again.

Soon the bus driver was on his feet too. The shouting

was getting louder, and the pointing worse. Only when the driver began to unlock the booth gate that kept him in did Dad stop. He backed away up the pavement, his finger still jabbing the air.

The driver held the bus, the door wide open, until Sean stepped aboard. The driver asked that question again:

'Are you just back from the war?'

Sean could not answer. He nodded, groping in his pocket for some coins.

'Don't worry about the money, pal. Wherever you're going today it's free.'

It was then that my brother cried.

Lie 39: I hate Dinah

Mum, because she was more comfortable with the public-school ideal, got to decide which one. Her choice for the next five years was Gordonstoun. Maybe she thought that counting the queen as a fellow parent would prove to Granny and Granddad that she had not married as badly as they thought. It was a decision confirmed when she toured the other option – Roedean. 'The girl who showed me round, would you believe, was barefoot!'

When I tell the story of those boarding years I moan about how I was dumped in the arse end of Scotland, completely on my own (Ed never counts). There was no one on my side. No one. Yet this is not strictly true. I had one unlikely sympathiser.

Ma Tait, who was one of the housemistresses. Some referred to her as Dinah. These names – the 'Ma' and the 'Di' – were how we tried to pick holes in her authority, and in our fear.

She was a small woman, thin and spiky, with short black hair and a voice that was easy to mimic. It had a posh grating quality, like the aunt in an Austen novel. Her own children had left home, and her husband too. She told me one Saturday afternoon that I did not need a man to get a lid off a jar. Just plenty of hot water.

Dinah drove her VW Scirocco fast, never giving anyone a lift. We watched her brake lights shrink ahead into the darkness, all of us hissing her off stage like a pantomime baddy.

One report reads that I do not concentrate, I am sulky, and I fool around. She uses the word 'sheep'. I was. Some mornings I was ordered to wait outside the staff room during break. She would appear, cotton wool in one hand and make-up remover in the other, and scrub at my eyes herself.

So I repeated often and loudly, along with everyone else, that I hated her, but this was not the truth. Later she would give me a copy of Anita Brookner's *Hotel du Lac* as a present, and pretend to overlook my persistent smoking behind the house. I was one of the few girls invited into her living room, where she made me tea and gave me cake. I suspect it was because she had glimpsed my world one Saturday afternoon in October 1981 and she never forgot it.

I had arrived at Gordonstoun with a brand new bike. A navy lady's model that, looking back, Dad hoped would give me the status his poor Irish background couldn't. It was a big deal and a 'monumental' expense.

An expense I parked in the bike shed. I had more important things to worry about. The new cohort of third-form girls were sorting themselves hierarchically, like grains of sand sliding through mesh. Within a fortnight my small self had been shaken down so far, the best I could hope for was that at breakfast the rest of them wouldn't get up and move tables as soon as I sat down. Desperate to fit in with the bikeless I pretended I had none. It sat in the shed.

By half term when Dad arrived to pick me up, I was exhausted. I had waited all month, through every hour and every minute, for him to come rescue me. But instead of a tour of the dormitory he jogged round to the back of the house, and to the bike. I trotted after him, dread sitting in my stomach like stone. The last time I'd seen it, the seat and one rear mudguard were gone, its carcass being dismembered one piece at a time.

When he reached the gloom of the corrugated-iron shed, I held back, eyes closed. But nothing dimmed the crash, or his terrible wordlessness as he threw one mangled bike after another out onto the path. Tangled they fell, kicking up dust, my insides heavier and heavier, a need to pee coming on.

And then he was out on the path himself, the unrecognisable piece of junk that my bike had become aloft in his hand. It had been reduced, like me, to its frame.

I would be lying if I recounted the words he shouted. I wouldn't even have remembered that same afternoon, my thoughts shrunk as they were to a white, hot panic. All I remember is the recognisable pitch of fury. Then his threat – he would be 'taking it up with Mrs Tait'. I remember too that I ran after him, begging that he wouldn't.

As we neared her door, Dad's rage made it impossible to repeat my plea. Instead I dogged him across the grass in silence, the corpse of my bike swinging loose from his hand.

When he stomped through her back door he broke up a parent–teacher meeting. A flustered couple dusted themselves down as they blundered out onto the path. We heard him through the windows and the walls, the other parents stumbling over the gravel, looking back. His bellows about the bloody waste of money, the extortionate fees, the incompetence, could be heard right the way over to where more parents slid from their Range Rovers and Jaguars, every head turned towards the Tait kitchen door.

Then there was the crash of my bike hitting her Formica island. I glimpsed it through the window, squealing the length of the worktop.

Perhaps as Mrs Tait contemplated the rageful immaturity of the man in front of her, she spied me hopping one foot to another outside, my arms flapping so hard it looked as though I'd take off. Because soon the shouting broke off, and from within the kitchen there oozed one of those rich, heavy silences that scares a child shitless. It was the last time Dad ever visited me at school.

Lie 40: There's nothing I can do

One of the clearest memories I have from Gordonstoun is an afternoon in the house television room. It is Saturday

and only the saddos are in there, still in uniform, hostage to
a daytime line-up of Premiership football or the black-and-
white film. I'm wondering whether to go for a ciggy before
the rugby match, or after, and whether I should ask Jane if I
can borrow her boots. I have grown increasingly ritualistic.
To concentrate on the detail means I don't have to worry so
much about the fact that there are still another eight weeks
to go.

Through the window, distantly, between the trees, I see
Ed walk past. It is autumn, red leaves carpeting the verge,
a wind blowing up the road. He walks into it, alone, his
shoulders round his ears, hands in pockets. It's only his
second or third week, and he looks so despondent, even
from two hundred yards, that I find it unbearable. I look
away.

My own boredom worries me as much as the boredom
of others. It is when the worst things happen. If I have a
ciggy before the match, I tell myself, and one after, then the
whole afternoon can be written off.

A couple of hours later and the school rugby match
is over. I've followed the first fifteen, clattering in their
boots, down the road from the pitch. Their legs and shirts
are caked with mud, breath clouding the air. They've won.
But instead of disappearing for my second ciggy Jane per-
suades me to accompany her. She tells me she needs to
pick up the boyfriend's rugby kit and wash it, and she
doesn't want to be hanging round the boys' mixed common
room on her own.

A boys' mixed common room is not somewhere I would
normally go. Though the furniture is the same as our own,

and the plumbing (which runs externally along the top of each wall), a boys' house is its own country. It smells of feet and damp clothes, the nylon-covered box armchairs ripped. We stand on the brown tiles, watching the boys drift in and out.

I can hear the gathering noise of something kicking off beyond the fire door. Jane, more used to hanging around a boys' house, moves over to a chair and falls into it. I look at my watch. The noise beyond the door sounds, on the face of it, like something is funny, and yet there's a tone to it which isn't.

'What's going on?'

Jane shrugs.

'We could go round by the pitches,' she says, 'and have a ciggy there.'

The door thumps open, and it is not a junior but the huge boyfriend, his hair wet from a shower, dirty kit clamped in his fist. Disappointed to find me there, he nods briefly in my direction. Then he throws himself into the chair beside Jane and pulls her onto his knee.

As they whisper to one another, I peer towards the door, which muffles a good deal of shouting. And laughing. It is the kind of laughing which speaks of someone having a terrible time.

Without warning, the door briefly bangs open, wide enough for me to see a senior leaning against the wall, a can of deodorant in his hand. He is yelling back up the corridor and it's then I see the distant line of smaller boys falling like bruised apples from where they've been hanging by their hands from the boiling pipes.

'What's with the deodorant?' I ask when the door bangs shut.

'What?' The boyfriend looks round.

'The deodorant.'

'It gives an impressive flame when you put a match to it?' He flaps his hand at me. 'It's just a game. You know, to see who can hang on the longest.'

I want to ask him if Ed is there. If Ed is amongst the small boys being tortured beyond the door. Yet to ask would be like gifting my brother a frailty. An interfering sister, especially one of my status, I tell myself, might put him in an even worse position. I am the very last thing he needs.

I smile at Jane and the boyfriend and retreat back outside, onto the concrete steps. The leaves snag amongst the grass and hedges as they fall. He probably wasn't even there, I tell myself, dodging away between the trees. I fall out of sight from the road and crouch down, rifling through the pockets of my coat. The cigarette lit, already I am wondering what's for supper and whether I have enough matches to last the weekend. There are many hours of it still to fill.

Lie 41: One day I'll report him

Ms Clough would sail up the study corridor, breasts thrust out ahead of her for balance, and try to catch us talking during prep. As tutor, the first appointment I had with her she told me that if I wanted to make a success of the opportunities school offered, whether that was being part of the hockey team or playing an instrument, then I must throw myself wholesale into Gordonstoun life.

Four years later, in both cases I had made no progress. Hockey required too much running around in the cold, while the clarinet needed reeds, which I could never be bothered to look after. They were often split and squeaky. Now almost as huge as her, I would turn up and flounder the half-hour on her sofa, careful not to raise anything controversial, like hockey, clarinet or even prep, where I was not getting much done either.

Even looking back, searching for characteristics, one grown-up human imagining the life of another, Ms Clough remains enigmatic. She loved the drama of a house search, sixty of us marooned in the mixed common room for hours at a time while she turned our dorms upside down. In the early days I shat myself. I knew I must be guilty. But the older I grew, and the more guilty I got, the less I worried. Worry was a luxury I couldn't allow myself. I needed focus.

Usually the crime was a stolen tenner, or a Walkman that had walked. Kleptomania amongst the rich was rife. But what a search threw up was never the stolen, only what was essential – cigarettes and booze.

The particular tutorial I'm thinking of, I can't remember how the subject of a rectal examination came up. Perhaps, when she asked, I told her the reason I hadn't practised the clarinet or made the hockey team was my stomach. I had blistering stomach pains, so bad that often I would have to lie down on the floor where I was.

'And you've been to see one of the doctors?'

'Yes.'

The first time I had gone out of choice, the second because I was ordered.

'And?' She peered at me, but I could not catch her eye. 'Come on, what did he say?'

'It's not appendicitis.'

'He gave you the rectal then?'

'Excuse me?'

'Did he put his fingers up your bum, dear?'

Ms Clough should have been an adult I could have talked to. Those tutorials necessitated many hours alone together, I adrift on her sofa trying to distract her from the fact I had achieved nothing since we last met.

But that afternoon, when we discussed the rectal examination, was the only time I remember revealing anything personal. When I nodded to her 'bum' question, Ms Clough struggled to hold back her excitement, pudgy hands clasped in her lap. Beyond the window three girls galloped through the silence, shrieking.

'How many times did he do it?' she asked.

'Twice.'

'Twice?'

She got up to stand by her desk, pushing aside pieces of paper, hunting for a pen.

'I've been doing a rectal audit.' She opened a small notebook and marked the page. 'When I've reached enough of a number maybe I'll report him.'

Lie 42: *That was entirely inappropriate*

Although infants do have memory, as we grow older we rarely recall those pre-verbal moments. It is as though we need to speak to remember. Before memories can be filed they need to be stitched into a story. Only then can they live.

Aside from language, what we need, in order to consolidate memories, is the ability to locate ourselves in the physical world. We have what are called 'place cells' in our hippocampus that allow us to form a cognitive map of the street, a familiar building, the position along the fence of a wooden stile. Exercising how we get from A to B, without relying on that irritating voice from the dashboard: 'At the next exit turn right,' helps us to locate both our memories and ourselves.

Nobel Prize-winners John O'Keefe, May-Britt Moser and Edvard Moser argue that what they call the 'mental travel' of memory is governed by our place cells. To know where we are may help us to remember who we are too. For instance, London cab drivers literally have more grey matter, because the ability to read a physical map influences the function and size of the hippocampus. When we give up our maps and put away our compasses, we could shrink the hippocampus into early dementia.

What's of more concern though is not whether I remember or forget, it is whether I indulge in fiction. Are these memories false? Did this tutorial really happen? Of course, I did have tutorials, but it is almost inconceivable that Ms

Clough would have discussed rectal examinations with me. There is no record of this conversation in my diary either. Can it really be true?

Some of us are easily led. Elizabeth Loftus, the psychologist who carried out the research into false memories that I introduced in Lie 2, is not interested in how we forget. She is interested in why we remember what never happened. One project in the United States found that 225 innocent people had been convicted on the basis of falsely remembered eyewitness accounts, convictions that DNA evidence later overturned. Loftus argues that memory is like a Wikipedia entry. We can go in and change it, but so can everyone else.

Always I have doubted this memory of the rectal, but I never spoke of it, and therefore it does not fall in beside Loftus's examples of being influenced by others. Along with T.'s birthday baths this was one of the first Lies that I wrote, and like his swims, I worried that I had made it up. Instead of being led by my audience, I wondered whether my audience needed memoir to be more miserable.

However, not even my fertile imagination could have come up with that phrase: 'rectal audit'. Nor had I thought there was anything wrong with the KY jelly or the snap of the rubber glove as the doctor lubed himself up. The humiliating discomfort of the procedure is now lost to me, but the strained view of the wall is not. I hunted it for something to fix on, its stains and marks, never imagining that he had his hand up my arse because he liked it. Without Ms Clough's audit comment, I would have remembered the rectal as a rectal, rather than as abuse. Which continues to be strange proof to me that our conversation must have happened.

Or did it?

In a fit of anxiety I assessed the sexual exploitation memories – T.'s birthday baths; his swims; the rectal – and then lobbed a question at the Gordonstoun Facebook group, regarding what I felt to be the least problematic memory of the three:

'Does anyone remember T.'s birthday baths?'

Perhaps I over-egged things by including the words 'dragging' and 'stripping'. Then waited.

Those people who had not been at prep school were disgusted, and in the vacuum created by their disgust a yawning lack of corroboration developed, which was soon replaced with fury. Those who had enjoyed school didn't like my memories at all. I had misremembered, and had been entirely inappropriate.

Three days passed.

Someone had to help me. Someone else must remember too. The birthday baths had really happened. I had not made them up. Finally, faced with a deluge of fury and denial, I utterly lost faith in myself. Even Violet couldn't say she remembered the baths when I asked. Being alone with a memory can be the loneliest thing in the world.

So I withdrew the question. In tears, I apologised profusely for misrepresenting T. If no one else remembered then I would have to accept that perhaps the birthday baths were a fiction. It was one of the most difficult apologies I've ever had to write.

Which may have been how it came across, because

within an hour Eva, who had lied on my behalf to get us both out of the naked swim, responded. She did remember the birthday baths, but felt there was nothing untoward in them. Then, completely unprompted by me, she asked whether anyone remembered T.'s swims.

To Facebook and this group, I became addicted. I had been scorned and saved in the same afternoon. Revelations of deviant behaviour on the part of both staff and pupils gathered. My sense that those school years had been all wrong was confirmed.

Lie 43: I'm going to kill myself

The first time I contemplated suicide my thought was to leap into the sea.

My grandfather had been transfixed by escape too, standing on the balcony of a lighthouse, telling his fellow keepers he could fly. I had no thought of flying. I had no hope. What I wanted was to jump.

You see, my mother had started delegating the more inconvenient parenting tasks to school. One letter reads: 'I am writing to the housemistress about your verruca and your teeth and hope that both of these can be dealt with, or at least a start made.'

At some point she also decided to stipulate a weigh-in. I was told to report to the Sanatorium each Tuesday morning. It was explained that my mother had noticed I had put on a considerable amount of weight. She hoped that regular humiliation (though I'm sure they must have phrased it differently) would keep my greed in check.

So on that first Tuesday I stood in front of the vast institutional scales, a gaggle of other girls with me. I would hesitate to call them friends. Moving through the crowd with her ledger, Matron made her way to the huge weight dial, its face orientated away from me, towards her.

'Go on then, step up,' she called over the girly din.

The mechanical clank of my step onto the weighing platform was met with a quiet hush. Every head tilted to watch the swinging arrow waver and waver, back and forth, back and forth, until it was still. Someone whispered:

'Fourteen stone.'

Recording this vast number in her ledger, Matron said loudly:

'Okay, off you get.'

There were other occasions when I must have gone to the San to be weighed, but neither Matron nor I had the appetite for it. Instead of diminishing my greed, Tuesdays intensified it. With each week the arrow sank deeper and deeper towards fifteen.

But it was the second act of parental delegation that nearly killed me. By then I was in the sixth year of the boarding-school experiment, an experiment that I felt wasn't working. I begged to leave. Begged.

There was a single payphone between sixty girls. Saudi Arabia was a long and expensive way away, so in the whole seven years I made only one call 'home', and this was it. I wasted it crying, too bereft to say anything other than repeatedly to ask if I could come home.

I have hunted this call down in my diary, but there are only oblique references, a panicked return call from my parents, and mention of a talk with the housemistress. All the entries leak despair.

Finally I was told that the headmaster wanted to discuss this request with me himself. The diary records two cancelled appointments, his secretary never offering an apology as I waited impotently at her desk. During that fortnight Dad wrote, the letter paper now grubby from reading.

'I would like you to stay at Gordonstoun (is that clear?) Only if you are very unhappy there would I think it a good idea for you to leave.'

He gives three examples of people who have become decent members of society despite being academic failures. Although my unhappiness and poor results are in the same paragraph he cannot seem to make any connection between the two. I am written off.

'O and A-Levels are not the B-all and end-all.'

He is right. They are not.

When the headmaster finally found the time to see me, I remember him as a small man, behind a big desk, wearing an insouciant smile.

'So Miranda, your parents tell me that you would like to move to another school.'

'Yes.'

'So which school did you have in mind?'

Fearful of the humiliation threatening at the back of my throat, I fixed my gaze on the pattern of his carpet, where countless boys had been beaten.

'I don't know.'

'You understand that you would still have to board?'

I said nothing.

'Are you listening to me, Miranda? I don't think you real-ise what a difficult position you are putting your parents in here.'

When I didn't answer again, he looked at his watch.

'So that's settled then. I'll call them in the morning.'

In the hours that followed I decided to throw all my books and then myself into the sea.

It was a mile or so from the school gates to the cliffs, between fields, along a straight track up to the brow of the hill. In my arms were the Arden *Othello* and *Hamlet*, the Lattimore translations of the *Iliad* and *Odyssey*, *A Passage to India* and the *Knight's Tale* (which was definitely going over the cliff edge first).

The day was grey, as school days often were, no cars on the Hopeman-to-Lossiemouth Road. On the other side a small wood had been planted. Tight up against the grass kerb stood sentry lines of young evergreens, their branches still near to the ground. It wasn't the best place for a cigar-ette, but since it would be my last . . .

Over the fence I fought with the needles of what seemed like a hundred Christmas trees and then gave up, still with-in sight of the road. It would have been a packet of Marl-boro or Camel that I carried in my Oxfam overcoat, because anything else was social suicide. I didn't have money for an acceptable lighter, so was always short of matches. In the wind I would have been going through them like a dog goes through his lunch.

In a pause between the furious scrape of a match and

its flame going out, I heard an adult-sized someone coming through the undergrowth, and in a burst of immortality struck the box again. Who cared? Dead, expelled, it was all the same.

The man bending through the trees towards me wasn't a teacher but a stranger – what every mother warns their children against. A local man in his twenties. He sat down and rummaged through his pockets for a hip flask and a lighter, as if I had been expecting him, and he me. Now I can only remember the brown of his jacket, and the warmth of his liquor in my throat. Leaning over he cupped the flame round the end of my battered ciggy. Then he lit his own.

I was fearful he would judge me for my acquired English accent. I wasn't sure I'd survive the humiliation of his disdain, for I already hated myself enough. Instead we talked, finishing his whisky and all the cigarettes.

The light had dimmed between the trees when I checked his watch for the time.

'It'll be tea soon,' I told him, suicide quite forgotten. 'I suppose I'd better be getting back.'

I turned to wave as I ducked between the fence lines, crossing over the road, my books piled in my arms. He saluted me once, disappearing back between the trees. Hope had arrived without my looking and stayed a whole afternoon.

Lie 44: It won't happen to my child

Charles Eisenstein, a radical economist, argues that corporate deceit, through advertising and branding, is destroying language. We are so used to the culture of ubiquitous lying, where America's navy is branded 'A Global Force for Good' and 'Freedom' is no longer something to strive for but a brand of shoe, that we no longer hear what it is that Donald Trump is saying. The tragedy is that even though journalists itemised every single lie during the campaign (which, by election week, according to Politifact, was a whopping 70 per cent of all statements made) we heard he was deceiving us, but no longer cared.

There is the institutional massaging of the truth that took us into war with Iraq, the lies that bankers used to fix Libor, the accounting fraud at Enron, or the silence that covered up the child abuse perpetrated by priests in the Catholic Church. But the institutional lies I'm most familiar with are those told about and by public schools.

Boarding as far as some psychotherapists are concerned is as harmful as being put into care. Almost all children who have boarded have at some point been abused, most often by those they were living with. Because as soon as a child arrives adaptation to the new regime must be swift. Some of us would have done absolutely anything to avoid the humiliation of being singled out.

Many of the boys owned weapons; air rifles, knives, catapults. Small boys were tormented by their seniors most evenings and weekends. The student-to-staff ratio at these times was sixty-five to one. Boredom is dangerous.

My diary narrates broken bras, ripped shirts. I can still remember trying to hold my skirt down while two boys tried to strip me. There was a kind of hate in it all – a frustrated fury with their own weakness. Stamped on, shot or tortured themselves, they would channel their hate at those smaller or frailer than they were. Invited out for a cigarette one evening I found myself on my knees, a boy's penis in my mouth. It wasn't rape. Merely submission. Everyone knew their place.

Some nights I would crouch beneath my desk with a copy of William Boyd's *School Ties*, reading the introduction over and over by torchlight. He describes his time at Gordonstoun with a comedic candour, and to my sixteen-year-old self it was rescue. Finally someone was telling the truth.

Yet even with this evidence of what was wrong in front of me I had no courage. Boyd's was a truth that felt too frail to share. I did not reach out to those more vulnerable than myself, or intervene as they were humiliated. It leaves me with a self-loathing that may never shift.

Our *in loco parentis* adults rarely interceded either. Public schools are their own country. In extremis some children were committing crimes so vile we didn't even hear they had been expelled. Nothing at all could be learned by their example. With an eye to the press, these children just disappeared.

The detail of what happened is immaterial. The more important question is, were we safe?

When I raise safety with Ed, he reminds me that although there were many air rifle incidents at Gordonstoun, the only time he was actually shot was at home.

By the time Sean fired on Ed, Sean had been boarding a year, at a school on a dead-end road, which led deep into Rannoch moor. A grisly Alcatraz, Rannoch School, facing rising debts, was finally closed down in 2002 after sex attacks among students began to be reported in the press. One ex-pupil told me that the only way to survive was by making himself sexually available to older boys.

Sixty-two leading independent schools have employed men who have been convicted of abusing children. Eton and Marlborough are amongst thirty where members of staff have been prosecuted for possessing child pornography. Gordonstoun as recently as 2010 sacked its maths teacher for downloading child abuse images, and is currently facing historical child sexual abuse allegations. One twelve-year-old girl was allegedly raped on a camping expedition by a member of staff at Aberlour, and a boy seriously sexually assaulted by another.

Surprisingly, convictions and allegations of this kind do not seem to have done any harm to school waiting lists, says Tom Buchanan, media consultant to a number of independent schools. 'I can't think of any school I've advised that has had a drop in numbers. This speaks to a generalised acceptance of there being a risk that goes with the territory. And of course parents always think it won't happen to their child.'

Lie 45: I am frigid

The Sunday afternoon I met Liza, I was interviewing to share a room in Drayton Green, London, W13. It was a room that had borne the brunt of a party the previous night. Liza picked her way through the party debris, wearing a pale blue kimono, and curled up on the sofa like a cat. She was beautiful and frail, wearing delicate Chinese slippers. Long fingers held the silk together at her throat, her hangover so acute I don't remember her speaking a word.

When I moved in a couple of days later the smell of party lingered, driven into the carpet, which was a curious pinky beige. The room was cut in half by the sofa. It and my bed acted as the seating area around a fireplace packed with empty Martini bottles, and the sturdy television set, balanced on a kitchen chair.

Liza and my new roommate, Samantha, were not like any of the girls I had left in Scotland. They could cook. Quietly appalled by what I ate, often they would urge me to try a new recipe or feed me sometimes themselves.

Perhaps it was their mothering that helped me shed the weight. Or simply that I grew lighter the farther from Gordonstoun that I fled. For years I had been wearing a first-class luggage allowance of misery. Now each morning that I woke in my seedy rented room it was with the enormous relief that I had survived. Without my trying, whatever it was that was bad about me dwindled slowly away.

Apart from dietary instruction Liza and Samantha introduced me to London, to marital alternatives, like having a profession, and to sex.

I had left school with the impression that I should not expect too much from it. It had never even crossed my mind to masturbate. In a dormitory touching yourself was unthinkable, the link to lesbianism clear. As far as I knew only one other girl ever had, and she was christened after a roll-on deodorant ('Mum') for her trouble. Bringing boys off was the priority, and any girl who wasn't interested was frigid. It's a word that Dad used against Mum, and a word that boys at school used against me. Being frigid felt far worse than any of the other things I had been bullied for – ginger; stupid; heavy. Gratefully, I speculated that in London frigidity would be something I could fix.

Samantha shared her bed with a boyfriend. The room she shared with me. Completely unembarrassed by the intimacy of this arrangement she expected me to be unembarrassed too.

Although I'd never had to share a room where sex happened, I had shared a room where there was crying, which is worse.

This lack of privacy was as familiar as no. 36's bulky payphone, which hung high on the wall at the top of the stairs. Like the one at school, the curly cord stretched and stretched, so you could sit on the floor outside the bathroom door with your feet pressed up against the banister railings, the whole flat able to hear every word. I still remember our number, because one of Liza's boyfriends, Kevin, always raced to pick up first.

'Sixteen forty-five,' he would shout in his midwestern American accent, 'and who may I say is calling?'

Kevin had arrived one Sunday afternoon, much as I had, but instead of interviewing, he came with his suitcase ready to move in. By Monday Liza, in her habitual kimono, looked as though someone had trodden dog shit into her carpet. Prior to Kevin the visitors to her room were nameless. She preferred to have two or three men on the go at any one time.

Kevin had shoulder-length, layered blond hair and ate 'Mac Cheese' cold and straight from the tin. One Saturday afternoon, with Liza and Samantha at work, he sat on the sofa, a creased Coke can in one hand, a crumb of Black balanced on his palm. Holding a match to the resin he hauled smoke through the metal into his mouth.

'So do you have a boyfriend?' he coughed, struggling to hold his breath.

'No. Not at the moment.'

'Do you want a boyfriend?'

I shrugged.

'Liza doesn't get me,' he exhaled. 'I don't know what's going on with her; what she wants.'

Though we had never discussed it I felt sure of what Liza wanted. For some time I had had an inkling that whatever was happening in the room next to ours, it was unsatisfactory. Right from my first evening at the flat, sitting in front of *EastEnders*, a Martini in one hand and a ciggy in the other, I had heard the shrill descant of Liza's sexual congress through the wall. Her cries followed a monotonous rhythm, each high-pitched mewl equidistant from the one before, and the one before that.

Samantha would get up from the sofa to raise the volume on the television, then sit down again without comment. But I could never concentrate. Every evening I waited for Liza to come. Always though, without crescendo, perfunctorily she stopped.

Innocently I lay on my bed later, mulling over her dissatisfaction. At least, I reflected, she would never have the ignominy of being called frigid.

Lie 46: Jesus knows best

We Tell Ourselves Stories in Order to Live is the title for one of Joan Didion's collections of non-fiction. We create our identity through the memories we store, rehearse and narrate. Our *self*-story is what defines us, but when we recount our stories we are often less interested in what is truthful than in what is tellable.

One of my stories was Liza. In fact the tales of Drayton Green have been told in pubs and at dinner parties countless times. Liza was a favourite. It served as an alternative *When Harry Met Sally* faked-orgasm-in-the-diner tale. Liza proved it didn't matter whether you faked it or not. Men did not notice.

Stories, like memories, solidify in the retelling, honed over years. They drift from fact into fiction. It is not so different a process for the novelist. Taking what is real and sculpting it so another kind of truth is written. Novels are liberated from reality to create worlds where the prose is clear and clean enough for us to see ourselves and our flawed humanity. We're only able to enjoy fiction, on the screen and between book covers, when we enter into the contract of falsehood knowingly. A story becomes deceit when we are not honest as we begin to tell. So the tales we share with one another, at home, at work and at school, are never untrue. We would be hounded out of the pub, the coffee morning and the playground if we made our stories up. Exaggeration is forgivable. But never an outright lie.

The philosopher and cognitive scientist Daniel Dennett

argues that if we're searching for the self in the brain, we are misguided. The self is a story that is drafted and re-drafted until it becomes a single narrative, one in which we are the 'chief fictional character'. We retroactively organise our lives through story, and we also tell stories that look into the future, the tales we force ourselves to live by.

My mother must have left finishing school with a particular version of her future in mind. Built on Christian mores, and held together with pins, her story struggled to accommodate the reality of her marriage. It wasn't a lack of financial independence that kept her trapped – she had enough cash to escape. What kept her cornered was her wretched story: the institution of marriage is more important than its individual participants and Jesus knows best.

I have no idea what her retroactive version of things would have been as she grew close enough to see how her own story would finish, but to live with it she needed, like so many of us, to have few regrets. Regret is about accepting fault. We are at most risk of regret when we have the most choices. Her story did not give her many. All choice had to be negotiated within the limited parameters she had given herself.

It is clear Mum's choices and the imagination she had to dream her story were stunted by gender and by class. The story I tell myself about my marriage and staying together happily ever after is a tidy one too. Infuriatingly it probably follows hers by rote. It is a tale that risked a deep structural edit in the hairy months of Mum's truth-telling. Dismantling Dad's story felt like trashing my own. It was clear I had shown terrible judgement, wasted years thinking my father was someone he was not. My credulity was painful. Whatever story I was telling lost its foundation. What was the point in throwing myself at some bogus tale about loyalty and mutual respect over a lifetime, when no one else was doing that? I had poured all my savings into Volkswagen shares.

What I didn't see was that loyalty and mutual respect had nothing to do with it. In their marriage something else was going on. Mum's conviction. My own. Dad's truth was one he was never allowed to own up to. Even if he had it was a version we would not have wanted to hear. We needed him to stick to the story. Our story. There was no place for running off to circuses or ditching marriages there. Compelled to keep up his side of things, there was nothing else for it but to lie.

Lie 47: This is the toughest letter I've ever had to write

When Dad cuts me off in a letter, he writes, as if it's never occurred to him: 'your mother keeps pointing out that your heart has not been in the course for some time.'

Which is true. I have spent a year on a BA in Library and Information Studies at Ealing's Higher Education College, which my father signed me up for in the week before the first semester started. It was one of the five courses he'd underlined with a red felt-tip in *The Times*'s Clearing List, speaking with the Admissions office himself. My A-level results had been disappointing. As soon as I found the college bar the slow slide into failure was secured.

Library and Information Studies was, as far as I was

concerned, beyond tedium and full of diligent people who were not clever enough to be anywhere else. It was a course, bar the diligence, I was perfectly suited to. My diary depicts a conspicuously tedious eighteen-year-old. As I wade through the pages for clues about her personality and motivation all I can think is: this diary needs burning.

I and a Goth from Swansea spent many hours casing our fellow students and many hours in the bar. One night a boy named Jacob staggered over. It was the red hair that drew him, and soon I was bent across his sofa, bewitched by the idea that I had a boyfriend who had both a motorbike and a drug habit.

Unfortunately it would be years before I realised that promiscuous is not the opposite of frigid. The opposite of frigid is aroused, and I did not find arousal here. Apart from missing almost every lecture, when Easter came I also missed the train home. I called Mum from bed, Jacob pretending to do a station announcement as he rolled the next spliff.

'Sorry,' I squeaked, 'there was a problem on the tube.'

It's a lie I remember because Jacob pushed me into it. Some years earlier I had given up trying to deceive my mother. Perhaps I hoped she'd come to a different conclusion about me than I had come to about myself.

However, the evidence was against me. Seven years of eye-wateringly expensive education had produced only one A-level pass – a C in Classical Civilisation. Neither had mixing with 'decent people' secured the prospect of a relationship with one. My mother had flushed her own prospects down the marital latrine, while I seemed to be casting myself into a toilet.

There is nothing whatever I remember about that year, other than the waste of it. While Jacob two-timed me with another redhead the entire twelve months, I failed the first-year exams and then I failed the retakes. The letter Dad sent was, in his own words, 'the toughest I've ever had to write'. He's cancelled the banker's order, and anticipates the Department of Education will be in touch for repayment. He tells me that I'm being cut off because he doesn't like to show favouritism. It has only been a couple of years since Adrian received the same missive.

Neither does he think there is any excuse for me refusing to live up to the Gordonstoun motto – 'showing that you can do it even if you hate it'. Which, although he has massively misquoted, is what school was like.

Then he gilds the 'cut' with the stories he likes to tell himself. The only reason that he stayed on in Saudi Arabia, he writes, was because we said we liked boarding. So my lies had convinced someone.

He acknowledges that the years apart have made it very difficult for us to live together. Apparently I'm at everyone's throats. Though of course I remember it as everyone else being at mine. Still he would like me to come 'home' and settle down to a 'sensible' way of life. Naïvely and movingly he writes: 'We could get to know each other a bit better and maybe become friends instead of all this fighting.'

I don't respond.

When he receives no acknowledgement of the toughest letter, he rings and asks again if I will move 'home'. I'm too distracted by Mum to answer. I can hear her voice, distantly at first, yelling from the kitchen: 'Go ahead and invite her, but I want nothing to do with it.' Soon she's on top of the mouthpiece. 'I do not want her home.'

Lie 48: I'll take her home

This has happened before and that's what makes it worse, my skirt up over my face in a single-bedded room. A dive bar on the Euston Road. I remember the deceit which led me upstairs by the hand. There was a view over the city to see.

On that occasion I blamed myself. The pub bouncer was a stranger, and I had been told not to go with anyone strange. I had also been counselled against bedrooms, for it was plain as the nose on my mother's face that this was the place where things *happened*.

But it's another story I need to tell. The one that is harder to put down.

I have a job in an interior design firm. Dropping out of college has led me here, as surely as the promise of a view. I am made Girl Friday. The receptionist, Gaby, is German and red-lipped. Often red-jumpered. She slams through the post each morning (because I cannot be trusted with it), a cigarette wagging between her lips. I am allowed a small perch behind her desk, an exposed and mean bit of melamine and a chair no one else wants. I shop and boil kettles, load envelopes, photocopy. In the evenings I tear across London to attend a secretarial course in a tired room on the Tottenham Court Road where the letters on typewriters have been blanked out.

Soon it is the Christmas party, and I don't remember much about the crawl along Victoria Street to the Buckingham. Gaby has peeled off to her 'good-for-nothing' husband. There are only a small number of core drinkers left. As the Rusty Nail cocktails are lined along the bar, I remember only the face of the publican, the shot glasses held between his bitten fingers, as he fills each one with liquid gold.

He watches me, knowing what comes after this.

Perhaps I know too, but the men I am with dare me to. And so the Nails are drunk.

Outside in the cold night a taxi is flagged and I am put into it with Mr Hancock, an architectural technician, who is also heading north. Hancock is a small, bespectacled man in his late thirties with thinning hair and a paunch.

As we weave out of Westminster it becomes Christmas Eve.

Mr Hancock pays for that long journey back into the depths of London, and as the cab steers east, and away from home, I am sobering to another ignored piece of parental advice. There is no such thing as a free ride.

The cab takes a right off the Edgware Road. The architectural technician mutters an inarticulate reassurance when I remind him where I live.

It is the first lie.

The rest of the journey is made in silence, the lighted streets winding past the window. Mr Hancock helps me from the car.

A dead relationship is written across his Walthamstow flat. There is much that is missing, the evidence of it boxed at the foot of the stairs. The sheets, when I find myself on them, are loose with sleep. Black dreams stink the pillow.

I am drunk.

And I am nailed.

And the 'No' I whisper makes his doing it bearable.

Once he has finished, he sleeps.

It is hours till dawn and I lie awake, too scared to find my clothes in the dark. Instead I lie in the dirty bed, his despair weeping between my legs.

He barely speaks when he finds me trailing around the filthy kitchen looking for a phone. And his silence is proof of my 'No'. He does not touch me again.

On the first day of January that the office is open, the reception area rank with stale cigarette smoke, Mr Hancock arrives, short and furtive. Before taking off his coat, he goes to the stationery drawer beside my desk and picks out a clean, white, self-seal envelope. And before dropping it on my desk he tucks something inside.

I hide it until lunch, for if Gaby sees it, she will take to it with her ash and her knife. The rest of the morning I hope that inside I will find a present, a small acknowledgement, a sorry. When Gaby leaves to buy her sandwich I open the envelope. All it contains is the plain white bra Mum bought me and a humiliation still difficult to voice.

Lie 49: I deserved it

The criminal justice system is an adversarial presumptive process in which it is assumed that at least one party is not telling the truth. The crime where this system seems to be failing us most is rape. An accusation of dishonesty is the only defence the guilty can furnish themselves with, and their barristers, with nothing else to go on, embrace this kind of argument with a desperation that is played out in long cross-examinations and an aggressive disbelief.

Ironically, for those who have been raped it has been hard enough to believe ourselves. Society has equipped itself with a surfeit of rape myths, which enable victims to accept what has happened to them by swallowing the idea that it has been their fault.

Under Section 1 of the Sexual Offences Act 2003, a rape is committed when a person intentionally, with his penis, penetrates another. It has to be a penis. The vagina was the only orifice of merit in the original Sexual Offences Act of 1956. It wouldn't be until 1994 that an amendment included the anus, and finally now we can mention the mouth.

This penetration must be without consent. The Rights of Women publication *From Report to Court* notes: 'It is always for the prosecution to prove that the complainant did not consent and that the defendant did not reasonably believe he or she consented.'

The reasonableness is an important word to those who have petitioned for improvements in the rate of rape conviction in the UK. As cited by Lord Falconer when petitioning for amendments to the Sexual Offences Act, in 2001–2 only 41.2 per cent of alleged rapists who were put on trial were convicted. He compared this with the figure of 73.4 per cent for general rates of conviction across all crimes. In his arguments he said that it was fair to expect a person 'to take care to ensure that his partner is consenting and for him to be at risk of a prosecution if he does not'.

Since the 2003 Act was passed, convictions have increased and more reported rapes result in prosecution. But still, only a very small proportion of rape cases that are reported to the police reach conviction, and 26 per cent of sexual offences that are reported are actioned as 'No Crime'.

Like many rapists, Hancock was an opportunist. He was like a burglar trying out back doors, hoping to find one unlocked. The intention was merely to get inside, but without any clear plan about which door to use. Opportunists are difficult to find guilty. The intention is diffused. In this scenario it's hard to prove premeditation, and after the burglary is completed there's no evidence of breaking and entering. Only leaking semen, and an inexplicable sense of shame.

In court, neither the defence team nor the prosecution is particularly motivated to understand what actually happened between complainant and defendant. Rather the system is organised in such a way as to establish winners and losers. It's a game in which the jury makes the presumption that when things kick off, it will be a fair and equal process, with both players starting from the same point on the board. But of course, like life, the criminal justice system is not fair. A well-financed defence team has more time and more resources at their disposal to win. But even without considerable cash behind him a rapist has a massive advantage. The victim is in the unenviable position of having to prove a case beyond reasonable doubt, while for the defence doubt is all that they need create.

Lie 50: Will you go out with me?

When they made their first reconciliatory visit, Mum and Dad were appalled by the keep-your-shoes-on-at-all-times living at Drayton Green. Immediately they put down a £3,000 deposit on a flat and guaranteed a mortgage. I was nineteen, with a salary of £8,000 per annum.

I found the flat on the A1, near to Muswell Hill, and to Violet. The Archway Road flat rumbled each time the Northern Line travelled north and south beneath it. A two-room bedsit, it crouched above an Asian newsagent, its windows facing east down Northwood Road. The night I got hold of the keys, I tore off my clothes and lay like a star on the empty floor. I was home.

The first evening Violet called round, the flat was still unfurnished, bar a second-hand fridge Dad had bought me and a Warren Evans double bed in pieces across the floor. It was already dark. She buzzed the intercom from the road, yelling up over the A1 traffic. She was in a rush.

I shouted back that I was still in my work clothes.

'You'll be fine.'

Down at street level her black Saab was thrown up against the pavement, hazard lights on, the Sisters of Mercy belting out the open windows. She hesitated when she saw my Laura Ashley pinafore dress, re-evaluating 'fine'.

Violet was the kind of Goth photographed by Japanese tourists. Her wardrobe was designer, her white warlocks from the best salon. She had transformed herself from the frumpy uniform-wearing Sloane that Gordonstoun was so good at producing into an angular beauty, both edgy and cool.

I collapsed into the passenger seat, the music on so loud we had to shout, and she took off, heading south. We were on a mission. She'd spotted a guy the night before, and she wanted to catch him. He would be in the Snatch, a new club at the back of King's Cross, she told me, and all I had to do was keep her company while we waited to see if he would turn up.

She parked down a residential street, perhaps Balfe or Northdown, and we wound down the windows, scouring the road for signs of a club. Last orders were being called in the pubs along Caledonian Road and soon a pair of Goths ambled past, disappearing into a lighted hallway between shop fronts. Stairs led down to a collection of domestic-sized windowless rooms, the DJ yellow-lit through a kitchen hatch.

It wasn't until one thirty that Violet's target arrived. With him was a friend, who had a menacing stillness about him, sharp cheekbones carving shadows beneath his eyes. Slowly he took in the room.

I watched him, like a mouse watches a cat. He took the seat beside me, leaning forward in his chair, elbows resting on his thighs. Violet pulled a scary face to the back of his head and gave her eyes a death roll. She yelled over the music:

'Don't look so fucking bored.'

This caught the cat's attention. Perhaps he knew the deal. Everyone knows the deal. The friend gets the friend.

He watched me. Then leaned over and shook my hand. I probably apologised for what I was wearing, for that is the kind of dismal start to a conversation I was capable of. Soon we fell into silence. I can still remember the discomfort of it, trying to seem engrossed in the music, my Laura Ashley pinafore as noxious as a fart.

As soon as I could I tried to escape, thinking that he might want to find someone more desirable. Instead he caught my arm.

Though he would ask the question and he would sleep with me often, we never did go out. Presumably because I was prone to wearing Laura Ashley, he preferred to turn up first thing on a Sunday morning and join me in my Warren Evans bed that he had put together himself.

Perhaps then it was the cat who gave me the human papillomavirus, or more likely it was the man before. The one who came when I was too drunk on Nails to refuse. Whoever it was, there was a lousy smear result, and then a stirruped visit to an outpatient unit on Holloway Road. Pants off I was asked:

'Are you sure you haven't had any warts?'

The doctor held a huge pair of forceps, eyes narrowed.

'Warts?' I asked.

'Yes,' his balding head disappeared between my knees, 'warts.'

'No.'

Though even now, Googling to find out what a genital wart looks like, I'm not really sure. Did I? Some pictures look horrible. My nether region was not something I knew much about, or took a lot of interest in.

'No. Never.'

'Hmm.'

There was the cold sensation of the forceps, and then the kind of inside hurt that feels as though the soul is being torn.

The laser treatment was a couple of weeks later. It was a fortnight in which I worked myself up into a lather. I had CANCER. (Or, though I never said it aloud, did I just have warts?)

Though Violet offered, it was Mum who came with me to the Whittington and waited outside as the abnormal cells were lasered away. Back home she tucked me up in bed. While we were out Dad had painted the entire flat, even the plug sockets, because nether regions were not his forte either.

Lie 51: Nemo me impune lacessit

My mother often told me that weddings were the best place to meet an eligible man. Tristan, whom I picked up at a Scots Guards nuptial, was a proof of principle and to her worth any disgrace. Dropping me off at the train station she was astute enough not to enquire where I would sleep after the wedding celebrations. All I had in my handbag was an empty wallet, my toothbrush and a clean pair of pants.

Googling Tristan as I write this, I find he's now CEO of an indeterminate financial company, which marks him out as the only solvent ex-boyfriend of mine from that period. Most of the others have gone on to become drunk, destitute or dead.

He was pale, his face eager, and the only 'date' we managed that winter was Disney's *Little Mermaid* at the Chelsea Cinema. It was a matinee. We sat at the front.

The rest of that autumn we held hands, arms locked at the elbows, his fingers so tight in mine my knuckles flared white. Nights, at Cavalry Barracks, we squeezed illicitly into mean army-issue beds, beneath scratchy blankets. Like

children we were beating back the chill of institutional rooms, shabby curtains and sixty-watt bulbs.

Then in the December of my twenty-second year Tristan was put on Royal Guard at the Tower of London. He and eight men were playing Grand Old Duke of York-type nursery games with keys, and presenting arms, and shouting: 'Who goes there?'

I was impressed. As was Mother.

What I regret most about Tristan, and would very much like to take back, is my ill-considered 'I love you.' Mum must have voo-dooed me into it. I could not have been in love by any stretch. It takes me years to work up to love, and even longer to admit to it. Anyway I was distracted. Besides Beef-eaters, mermaids and single beds my diary narrates an un-tidy closure with a bass player recently signed to Elektra, and intermittent phone contact with a drunk I'd hooked up with on Camden Town's Barnet-bound platform. It also tran-spires I couldn't invite Tristan round to my flat because a baggage handler from Luton had moved himself in the week before (a 'totally platonic arrangement', one entry reads).

But my mother and I kidded ourselves that the only thing going on was a uniformed second lieutenant on Royal Guard Duty at the Tower.

The night of the Ceremony of the Keys and Who-Comes-There, two other officers and Tristan's sister joined us for whisky in his quarters. It was a flat with ruched curtains and the pervasive stink of prep schools and torture that haunts much of the upper classes.

We waited for the goose-stepping up Water Lane to begin, the shouts to a Yeoman, the safe keeping of keys; a cere-mony which has begun every evening for centuries at ex-actly seven minutes to ten. We waited. Tristan's men laid on more whisky, and more, so by ten to ten he was very much the worse for wear, his bearskin askew.

Beyond the Tower walls the city had emptied. Gathered on the cobbles the night felt to me colder and blacker than any other corner of London. I wanted to go home. It was a long way, and I was still in my clothes from the previous night.

We stood on the Broadwalk steps flapping our hands against our sides in the cold, with the small band of red-coated Guards at attention outside the Queen's House. In the darkness came the clang of the gates, and the shout of the sentry along Water Lane.

'Who comes there?'

And the Yeoman's answer: 'The Keys.'

The boots of the Warder and his military escort echoed along the cobbles, up under the Bloody Tower Arch till they were beneath the steps.

Tristan bellowed some incoherent orders, the December air clouding in huffs around his face. Wobbling on his about-turn, he provoked tuts from the Freemen of the City. One hissed: 'Drunk!'

The keys were marched to the Queen's House and over the wavering call of the bugle the Freemen filed off.

When we called by the flat to say goodbye, Tristan already had his bearskin off, the buttons on his tunic wrenched undone. He was bent over the laces of his boots.

Tristan hated to be left. When he was in barracks, although it was forbidden, he would beg me to stay. He was like the small child abandoned in a chilly prep school, desperate for his mother, and every other institution that followed mirrored the abject loneliness of the first. His pleas for me to stay woke the buried child in me. I did not care that I might be caught.

But the Tower was different. No woman stayed overnight. It was completely beyond the pale. For twelve hours every night, ten to ten, the Crown Jewels and their guards were, and are, locked in. Nothing transgresses this rule.

Tristan, drunk, pulled me down beside him, pleading in

whispers, his eyes on my shoes. Bereft at the thought of a night alone he did not notice the uncomfortable departure of his sister and the two other officers, nor the clangs and jangles of the Tower going into lockdown for the night.

It says in my diary that I ran him a bath. That we shared it, and slept.

It was five forty-five when I woke, dawn still a long way off. Two hours till the office opened, a tube ride away in Bloomsbury, four until the gates unlocked. Again he pleaded. Please, please would I remain until the Tower was opened to the public at ten?

To save my job I couldn't, and by ten past six on that December morning Tristan, on guard at the Tower of London, was back in uniform. Alone he marched me down towards Water Lane, a grave silhouette in front. His platoon, on guard, whistled in low tones as we passed, the darkness colder and blacker even than the night before.

At the first gate, beneath the Byward Tower, Tristan knocked on the door, rousing a furious Beefeater. I remember only a huge brass plate: 'Yeoman's Gaoler', and his quantity of keys. Tristan gave an exaggerated salute. Then we bent beneath the slender rectangle of door in a massive gate, our line expanded to include the Yeoman of the Guard. I was marched over the stone bridge to Middle Tower. No word passed between us, Tristan standing to attention as the keys were inserted in the final lock and the handle turned. It was only when at last I struggled through the second cutout door onto Lower Thames Street that I heard him murmur to the Beefeater:

'I found her with one of the men.'

Lie 52: I'm Sylvie

I volunteered with the Samaritans. I had known despair.

The Enfield, Haringey and Barnet branch knew despair too, and was manned by a humane collection of those who had met misery and knew its colours. One of the volunteers wore only purple, in cascading shades.

I was twenty-one, and manned the phone on regular evenings and weekends, with a commitment of one full night a month, 10 p.m. until 7 a.m.

The branch was based in a Victorian semi, round the corner from Bounds Green tube. In the bay-windowed front room there were three telephones in booths, a scraggy nondescript blue carpet worn threadbare beneath three cheap office chairs. At each desk sat a curly corded phone, with pull dial, and a big handset that could be jammed comfortably between shoulder and ear. The chairs were on wheels so that we rolled between the desks for biscuits, exchanging cryptic notes: 'TEA! TWO SUGARS' or 'ANOTHER BRENDA?'

Before my time, a volunteer was able to ask those who wanted to masturbate if they would prefer to avail themselves of a service. The code question was: 'Would you like to speak to Brenda?' However, Brenda had thrown in the towel by the late eighties and we were left to fend for ourselves. I did not fend well. Evenings and weekends obscene phone calls were almost all I got. I was young and female, and callers would hang up on the men and older women so as to do it with me.

We were only allowed to terminate calls if we were sure they were 'abusive', and we were encouraged to ask every caller: 'Are you feeling suicidal?' I would try to ruin their orgasm with the suicide question, whilst they attempted the soundless come.

Although the overnight stints were exhausting, during those hours, between ten and seven, the wankers fell off and despair began calling. As night dragged towards dawn their loneliness swelled. A widower lost in his empty bed, the single mother up for eviction, pensioners facing Christmas, the teenager too scared to go home.

By four, when the night was at its coldest, my teeth ground hollowly, the bitter taste of emptiness in my mouth. I was often so tired it sickened me, dozing to the second volunteer's soft 'mmms' and 'yeahs' as she listened through the small hours to a mind turn endless circles. It was in this late part of the night that Sylvie rang.

I picked up the handset, blundering over to a booth.

'This is Miranda.'

A terrified voice whispered:

'I'm Sylvie.'

'Is everything okay?' There was silence. 'Sylvie? Are you okay?'

'He's coming,' she said. 'Can you hear?'

And I could, the regular thump of a shoulder thrown against the door. As the wood was pounded into its frame, we murmured to one another, crouched against what would happen when her lover broke in. He was coming, she repeated, and I lied to reassure her, as sure as she that he was.

The lover stopped hurling himself at the door and took to shouting through the letterbox. Then he disappeared to rouse his mother for the key. In the long quiet that followed she told me the sorry things that had happened on previous nights. We whispered together, terrified, her hauling me through scene after scene, in bedrooms, in cupboards, beneath stairs, until a grey light crept round the cheap cotton curtains, and the birds of Bounds Green woke.

He was coming, she said again. She heard his tread on the stairs.

And soon he was, his breath ragged, his cackle as sick as the Joker's, her desperate voice disappeared.

A long, frightening silence followed and then, like the harsh dring of a call in the night, she snickered into the phone extension, her scorn deteriorating with measured slowness.

Sylvie laughed at me. And laughed.

Afterwards, on the street outside, not yet able to face the tube or the day, I stood and stood on the pavement in the queasy orange light.

Lie 53: I want a relationship

Henry, my counsellor, was in his sixties. He counselled out of a room in Finsbury Park. I remember the chairs, the carpet and the walls being entirely brown. I had come because a fellow volunteer at the Samaritans had taken me aside and offered to pay. Not seeing what a shambles I was in, I reasoned that the only problem I had was men. They were all bastards.

When Henry asked me what I wanted to get out of our sessions I replied:

'A relationship.'

'Presumably a long-term relationship?'

I nodded, tearful.

'Are you in one at the moment?'

'Yes.'

'Tell me about him.'

Rich was a nineteen-year-old mental health nurse at a North London psychiatric hospital, with a sister and mother who disapproved of me.

'And how old are you?'

'Twenty-three.'

'So how long do you estimate this relationship will last then?'

'A year.'

'Because your relationships usually last that long?'

'No, not really. Some have, but never in a single sitting.'

'Okay, but you think this one will last a year.'

'I want it to.'

'Well, a year seems pretty optimistic to me. At his age, I don't imagine you'll get past the summer.'

Appalled, I stared out the netted window to the street. Neither of us spoke for some time.

As it happens Rich and I lasted barely another fortnight. One of the reasons might have been that I had not been entirely honest. Rich wasn't my only relationship. I didn't mention the estate agent I'd been at school with, or the Irish hairdresser with a heroin habit.

I didn't mention them because they didn't count. Frankly I'd probably forgotten them myself. When Henry asked, the nineteen-year-old militant vegetarian working the wards of North London was the only man I wanted.

Yet Henry had hit a nerve with his quip about the summer. I was not two-timing Rich out of greed, but because I was hedging. To minimise the opportunity for rejection I had spread myself thin and wide. I no longer had to worry about trusting anyone else, because they sure as hell could not trust me.

Perhaps it was also about not being able to end a relationship. The guilt ate me up. It was easier to get caught out for philandering than confess I had moved on.

I use the term relationship loosely. Every man I went to bed with I wanted a relationship from. The hairdresser and I had been trying to pull off something long-term for two years, but smack was an obstacle too difficult to scale. He and I couldn't even talk about it. He'd told me the aluminium foil lying around in his bedroom was for dyeing his clients' hair. But I couldn't give him up. I'd developed a habit too – for the way I laughed in his company. Whole mornings would pass when I did little else.

Although I told Henry about the hairdresser's heroin addiction, the detail I kept to myself. Instead I started writing him unsent letters outlining that I never wanted to come into his brown room again. Face to face I tried to fob him off with news of the estate agent, but Henry wasn't easily fobbed. He wanted me to take the gear seriously.

'I'm sure he's only smoking it,' I said when an AIDS test was mooted.

If anyone asked why my relationship with the hairdresser ended, I always blamed smack. It still remains a convenient excuse. More problematic, the diary reveals, was my dishonesty. That was why the hairdresser pulled away. He had found evidence of another man – 'the pair of biking boots in the hall and on the underside of the loo seat, one sodden black pube'.

In my diaries I find I have been loyal to no one. And though I blame men for not ringing, for not wanting a relationship, it is me who cancels dates at the last minute, or tries to squeeze two into one afternoon. The worst of it is my behaviour comes to me as some fresh revelation. It is excruciating to realise, in the light of my unwillingness to forgive my father, that I was so faithless myself.

By session eight with Henry I had grown to loathe his grouchy truth-telling. He had sniffed my dishonesty and gave me a task that he hoped would expose the root of my lies.

Henry asked me to write an honest letter to my parents. I've kept many of my unsent letters, often to boyfriends, but that letter is nowhere to be found. I remember the struggle to write it, how meagre it looked on the page, how much I'd still not been able to say, and Henry's unenthusiastic response.

'Do you think you're protecting them,' he asked, 'by not writing down the feelings we've discussed together?'

When I wouldn't or couldn't answer he would always leave an uncomfortable few minutes' silence for reflection before picking up his monologue again.

'What do you think would happen if your parents were to hear how you feel?'

I shrugged.

'Do you think they're going to be racked by guilt? Be sorry? Be too fragile to take it? Or do you actually suspect they're not going to react at all?'

I gritted my teeth.

'You may pretend that you're protecting them, but I think the only person you're trying to save here is yourself.'

Lie 54: I just wanted to return his pullover

I had been single since Sunday and it was already Good Friday, my ex's boots still planted beneath the bed. In *Time Out* there was a three-starred gig listed at the Monarch. I preferred to drink elsewhere, but I thought I should find more original reasons to go into Camden other than getting laid. I had just finished my last session with Henry, where we had gone over again (as we did each week) the necessity for honesty in a relationship, and keeping my knickers on. Therefore my tentative resolve that evening was to remain sober and fully clothed.

As soon as I got inside the pub I saw him. He was sitting at one of the large tables near the door, still almost a boy. I remember nothing of what he wore – perhaps it was the purple T-shirt or the cropped ex-DDR coat that I can recall from other memories. He had brown eyes in a clear face.

I went over to the bar, as was my habit, and ordered a pint. The pub was crowded, the corner given over to a tiny stage. A couple of musicians were arsing about with their equipment. After a while they started to play.

Soon a Goth with blotchy eyeliner got chatting. Perhaps he offered to buy me a drink. I never accepted drinks. Sean had taught me that accepting drinks was falling into debt. And for that kind of debt the bailiff always called.

I humoured the Goth, my eyes shifting to the table and the boy. He dutifully paid attention to the band, a half of Guinness sitting in front of him, barely drunk. Occasionally he leant over the table and nodded at the person opposite. A man.

The music gave the Goth the excuse to lean in close and shout, his beer sloshing between us as he emphasised each of his points. The first act wound up to desultory applause. Five minutes passed, all of us more interested in the empty stage than we had been when it was filled. Still the head-line band did not appear; my mind worked through possible pick-up strategies.

'There's someone bothering me at the bar,' was what I said when I went over. 'Do you mind if I sit down?'

The boy with the cheekbones smiled, his friend shuffling along the bench. The friend introduced himself as Arnaud, and the boy as Matthias. Where were they from? I asked.

'France,' said Arnaud, indicating himself. 'And Germany.'

Germany? I'd laid a heroin addict, a bedwetter and an alcoholic, but a German? There was also a hostile, self-assured quality about the friend, as if he knew the world and was tired of it already.

Matthias, my target, said nothing.

I watched the empty stage, wondering how to extricate myself. As I prevaricated, we were forced to listen to a good deal of Arnaud's complaints about England. Matthias said little, his face set in an unflinching smile.

Arnaud disappeared to a phone box, leaving his charge alone. I insisted on another Guinness, and plenty of cigarettes. I probably also plied him with one of my rehearsed monologues – perhaps the one which involved a sadomasochistic neighbour who enjoyed hooking up her boyfriend to the car battery. Before a man took advantage of me I always liked to test his courage.

The boy continued to smile.

Arnaud returned. He was flustered. There was a great deal more fretting, this time over a toothbrush. Arrangements he had made to stay with someone's mother had broken down. With each word their worlds and mine strayed farther and farther apart.

But despite his references to mothers and toothbrushes, perhaps I offered to let them sleep on my futon. They were children. Over-educated children, one doing a PhD at Cambridge, the other a non-specific postgraduate humanities degree.

Still exercised about the toothbrush and the absent band, Arnaud ordered us out of the Monarch and on to Bar Gansa on Inverness Street with its red awning and greying goose. It was on the way, sobering to the North London night, that I finally admitted that I was a secretary. Which led, over coffee, to Arnaud and I having a fight about Sartre. I said goodnight.

Reaching the top of the escalator in Camden Town I

remarked to myself that I had maintained my resolve. It was the first time in a long while that I had arrived in Camden and left it both sober and alone.

The exhilaration lasted only as far as Archway, when I began to regret having no way of getting in touch. But the boy was German, I repeated. Asking for a number would have looked desperate. What I needed was a long-term relationship and this definitely was not it.

Yes, I threw myself in front of the television, it was a relief. He was German, and small. I'd always seen myself with someone bigger. Christ, he was a scientist too. I lit another cigarette. There was nothing redemptive about any of it. He lived in Cambridge. The countryside.

When I check my diary for movements over that Easter weekend, I find that Henry's counselling had not had the conclusive effect I have pretended to myself. The relationship break-up was not going as cleanly as I would have liked, and to console myself I had hooked up with another ex.

Mess and sex aside, by the Tuesday I had made a decision.

I rang up Directory Enquiries from work and asked for the number of the University of Cambridge. The French sidekick had mentioned the Zoology Department.

'Good morning,' said the receptionist.

'Morning. I wonder if you could give me the address for one of your PhD students. He left his jumper in the pub on Friday, and I wanted to post it back.'

It was Gillian, my colleague, who suggested the jumper. A perfect lie. A jumper was just the sort of object Cambridge University students might realistically leave behind them – or did 'pullover', I wondered, seem more authentic?

'His name?'

'Matthias Landgraf?'

'How are you spelling that?'

'I'm not sure.' I heard her riffling through the pages of the directory.

'Like I say, I just wanted to return his pullover . . .'

'Landgraf, did you say?'

'Yes.'

'Just putting you through.'

In the bowels of the Zoology Department a phone rang and rang and rang. Eventually a woman picked up.

'Hello?'

She sounded right in the middle of something very important.

'Can I speak to Matthias Landgraf please,' I managed to ask.

'Matthias? I'll just get him.'

There were rushed footsteps and a fire door banged. It was only when I heard someone coming back through it that, heart hammering, I hung up. Gillian hissed from her desk beside me.

'And?'

'I hung up.'

'Did you get his address?'

'No.'

'So what are you going to do now?'

Gillian, pushing forty, still lived at home with her parents. This fact I repeated to myself so as to get up the courage to ring the receptionist back.

The second time I asked simply for the Zoology Department's address. But then I couldn't resist lying again in my letter to Matthias. I wrote saying that I would be visiting Cambridge to meet a friend (though I knew no one between Mill Hill and the Scottish borders). Could he do tea?

I arrived at Cambridge station to find he was late, jogging up the street towards me, wearing, this time, I'm fairly positive, his purple T-shirt.

I often say to myself and to others that Henry was the significant factor in my falling in love with him, which overlooks an obvious truth. That Matthias is a man worth falling in love with.

What he remembers is the ducks on the Mill Pond. Although I have only the vaguest memory of ducks, my diary entry speaks of them too. It is the moment he recognised that I might be what he was waiting for. I am less tender, moaning on in my diary, and to anyone who was prepared to listen, that despite the fact I was carrying a spare pair of knickers and a toothbrush, he put me on the last train home.

Lie 55: Honestly it won't be so bad

White lies do not injure anyone, are morally neutral and, many would say, trivial. We could argue then that the pullover lie is a white one. Pullovers don't injure anyone and they have no effect on our morals. In fact without the pullover Matthias would have ended up with another scientist

(he never got out much) and then killed her career. Repro-
duction is a straightforward way that male academics can
take out the competition. So it's not just a white lie but a
very good one. However others would say the pullover is
neither white nor grey, nor even good. It's merely gratuitous.

Justifying to ourselves that a lie is necessary, or in the recipient's favour, is something we do every day. That dress is
lovely; I'm very happy for him; it was absolutely fine; your
child was no trouble; honestly it won't be so bad. These are
the currency of every day. A whole story crouches behind
each one.

These kinds of lies are standard amongst medics. They
know from experience that we're easily deceived. Yellow
pills make depressed people feel better, and sleeping pills
need to be blue. Large pills seem more effacious than
medium-sized ones and the very tiniest pills work best of
all. Ninety-three per cent of UK doctors admit to conduct-
ing non-essential examinations on patients, and 97 per cent
report that they have prescribed placebos at least once in
their career. They do it because feeling cared for works. In
one experiment two hundred patients suffering from irritable bowel syndrome were put into three groups. The first
were told they were on a waiting list, the second given per-
functory sham acupuncture, and the third 'very schmaltzy'
sham acupuncture. Of the three groups the over-schmaltzed
did best.

Children learn quickly that white lies are necessary.
When seven-year-olds were asked to take a photograph
of someone sporting lipstick on her nose, most lied when
asked: 'Do I look okay for the photo?'

In a later study a similar cohort, when given a bar of soap as a present, pretended, quite spontaneously, that they liked the gift. White lying knits us together with those around us. When we empathise with one another we find it easier to know what it is that the people we care about need to hear. Who wants to know and does it matter that the new dress is hideous, or it wasn't a lovely evening at all? To always tell the truth shows a disregard for other people's feelings that can leave us without friends.

In fact the closest relationships we have are the ones in which we lie the most. We tell our lovers that they are the best and the biggest and that the number of other men before them is at most one or two. We tell our children that they're brilliant, that they do fantastic drawings of dinosaurs, and that when the nurse presses a needle into their arm it really won't hurt. We tell ourselves that these lies have an altruistic motivation, though dinosaur admiration prevents another boring request for biscuits and the true figure of previous sexual partners is, for my own part at least, too difficult to admit.

Lie 56: We're spending quality time together

One year I gave Dad, for his birthday, a copy of Blake Morrison's memoir *And When Did You Last See Your Father?* I wanted him to read the narrative that came closest of any I had found to capturing his character. Morrison reveals a duplicitous and unfaithful parent whose personality is as much camouflage as distraction.

Although I didn't realise it then, Dad must have rec-ognised himself and panicked. It had happened before. A few years earlier the book had been J. R. Ackerley's *My Father and Myself*. On the inside cover, in black ink, Dad has written: 'Ed said you wanted this one. I hope there's no parallel with us. I haven't got a second family hidden away. Honest!!' (But only because Mum had insisted on a vasectomy in 1971.)

However, in both cases he needn't have worried; with Morrison's father it was the personality I recognised rather than the crime.

I had found a copy of the book in Dillons on Gower Street; I spent many of my lunch hours there escaping from the architectural practice where I worked. The book was a present I innocently gave many people that year, as though I'd found a key to my father, a secret that everyone needed to hear.

I sent the book to Dad in Scotland with the inscription: 'to forgiving the past', (meaning maybe he should forgive that big lie of his mother's) but he must have wondered if I was onto something else. Presuming himself rumbled he threw out an invitation. Through Mum he made the request that before Matthias and I were married he and I 'needed' to have one last weekend together.

By the time I agreed to go it must have been about May or June. The days were long and dry. Dad had booked the two of us into the sort of hotel where you dump a mother-in-law for Christmas. It was situated within coughing distance of

Junction 2 on the M6. We were the only guests.

I drove up on the Friday evening. At best I was an extremely nervous driver. It had taken five tests for me to pass, and that evening I was barely able to turn out onto Archway Road without breaking into a sweat. I could kill people. When I drove I had to wind all the windows down and put the stereo on full blast. I held the steering wheel so tightly my knuckles went white.

Exhausted, I must have arrived about eight o'clock.

'Great hotel,' Dad shouted from the door, as I lumbered towards him, dragging a bag. 'And we've got it all to ourselves.'

I had always been wary of being in his company. Things had grown better but they were not fundamentally changed. For instance, a year or so before this dreaded weekend in Warwickshire, he had picked me up from Glasgow Central train station. One minute he was boring the pants off me about a situation at work, and the next he was out of the car. Leaving his door wide open, he strode round to the vehicle in front. It was a Vauxhall Corsa filled with teenage boys. As he shouted they peered up at him through the bleary condensation-covered windows. Their passivity must have infuriated him. Soon he was striding round to the bonnet to hammer the windscreen with his fists.

I imagined, from my sightline, over the lip of the dash, that someone would inevitably get out and belt him, but maybe they realised he was dangerous, because as soon as he took a step back, the Corsa squealed away, all the windows tightly closed.

When he returned to the car he said nothing, a cacophony

of horns blaring behind us. The lights had long turned green.

More often, though, my anxiety was just about not know-ing what to say. The black silences he had inflicted on us over the years had choked all memory of a relaxed conver-sation. I would dread finding myself alone with him – that he would not 'be speaking', as my mother termed it, and that I might be the cause. But this anxiety tells you much more about my personality than his. Dad was as much a talker as he was a sulker. Perhaps it was down to his deteri-orating hearing. Unable to distinguish what other people were saying it felt safer to control the conversation himself.

That Friday evening, before I was married, I found him in a buoyant mood, which gave me enough latitude to won-der why on earth I had ended up in a dingy hotel on the M6. Slinging my bag onto the nylon bedspread I was dubious.

I joined him for a safe supper of meat and potatoes in a deserted dining room. He talked as though he needed to fill in every crevice of silence, with the fervour of someone who had a fear of it. At one point there must have been a pause, long enough that I was able to retreat to bed. As we headed upstairs I thought that by remaining in bed most of the morning I could safely kill half a day, but as we reached our adjacent doors he reminded me that breakfast would be served between eight and nine.

'I'll see you downstairs about half past.'

I lay in bed wondering what I was there for. What did he want?

The rest of the weekend was spent walking in circles through humdrum fields, the distant roar of the M6 to our backs. Dad talked and talked, skirting whatever it was he might have wanted to say, his anxieties opaque. Perhaps like a poem his intention needed the care and patience I was too distracted to give. Or perhaps he was kicking around the Warwickshire dust wanting only to reassure himself that I had not yet found him out. Or perhaps, with the stink of his panic so bad, he had woken up to the fact that marriage wasn't a suitable ambition for anyone, especially when there is the risk of winding up hostage to a man like himself. But none of this translated. He had given himself the opportunity to tell the truth. A whole weekend of opportunity and though he had talked without pause he said nothing.

Lie 57: Marriage is all I want

It was 1996. My mother and I had spent a long day trying to choose me a wedding dress. It was a day that had started with hope. Shopping and marriage were a great combination. To everyone's relief a husband had been found.

By late afternoon we were in the bridal department at Liberty, which was then situated on the top floor. The last dress I'd had on was a Jasper Conran, with a £2,500 price tag. It was the dress Mum wanted – huge amounts of tulle, and extremely white. Maybe I'd had too many cups of coffee, maybe I had PMT, or maybe I just wanted her to back off. This was *her* dream, I was beginning to realise. Not mine.

Whatever the reason, I felt an overwhelming urge to kill her. To nudge her over the atrium banister in Liberty and watch her tumble head first into the accessories department, and those endless bins of peacock-printed scarves.

Throughout my childhood, marriage, even ironically for my mother, was The Panacea. In our home, it had always been clear that a woman's place was on her back. On one occasion I rang Dad to ask his advice on pensions, and he told me to 'marry one'. There seemed to be no Plan B. Yet when I produced Matthias at a family weekend, he stared over Matt's shoulder, as if by not acknowledging him, he could make his replacement disappear.

Clearly, none of the women on either side of the family had made good decisions with regard to marriage. And given that it was the only career decision that they were in a position to make, these were choices that became difficult to live with.

Granny, having ended up as Mrs Ian Paterson, complained copiously about everyone else's choices, often with good cause. The bad decision-making had continued with my mother. I have a letter from Dad dated June 1985, which reads: 'Mum and I had a terrible lunch yesterday with your Gran! The lunch was okay but she was awful – reminding me in particular that in her opinion, and her late husband's, I was not a fit person to marry their daughter.'

As the only girl, it was made clear to me that someone finally needed to get it right. Granny wrote in 1987, the year before I left school: 'Here goes wishing you all the best in the world and a tall handsome and wealthy husband (later).' In another letter Granny told my mother not to worry. She'd been 'man daft' too.

I see now that rather than being 'man daft', I was focused. Everyone had given me a clear career path. I needed a husband, and I needed one fast.

That afternoon at Liberty's, I don't think my mother's own tricky marriage was the reason I wanted to tip her over the banister. Maybe I had smelt her overwhelming levels of desperation and self-deceit and couldn't quite imagine how she thought it a good idea to sell me down the same river. Was that all I was good for – dresses and divorce?

Or perhaps what enraged me was simply the enormous price tag. Not that I remember being particularly moral in that regard. If it had suited me to wear a huge dress costing the equivalent of a lifetime of antiretroviral therapy for two children, then I'm sure I would have gone for the dress.

I didn't. I went with a dressmaker who designed something simple. The material wasn't as white as Jasper Conran's, but a gunmetal organza, and to my mother's eye, when she received the material sample, grey.

Twelve weeks before the wedding, and after a good many prayers, she rang and asked me if I'd had a look at the organza.

'No. Why?'

'Go get it and have a look.'

'Why?'

'Just go and get it out the bag.' She sounded excited. 'My bit's discoloured.'

'Discoloured?'

'It's rusty. Maybe?'

'Maybe because you've been keeping it on the bathroom windowsill?'

'No. Actually, Miranda, I kept it in my sewing box. Well, are you going to go get it?'

'No. I can't,' I lied. 'It's already with the dressmaker.'

'Well, if I were you, I'd ring her up ASAP. Make sure it's not happened to your bit too.'

I reassured her that while her sample had come from a shop on Berwick Street, the material for the dress was purchased from her faithful and favourite John Lewis.

'It'll be fine,' I said.

But it wasn't. When I dragged the bag out from beneath the bed, the organza looked as though a cat had pissed all over it, the stain leaking through its folded layers in a huge round rusted mark. The lady at John Lewis said she'd never seen anything like it.

In the end, like Mum wanted, I wore white.

Lie 58: We parent together

I'm pregnant. It's a mistake. Matthias wows about the new brand of non-latex condom – 'for that natural feeling'. He is right. Natural, but only because it's split.

Without the courage to take a test, I drink loads in the lead-up to Christmas, hysterical. And smoke industrial quantities, as if either of these things might make the still fictive 'it' go away. At some point in that dead time between Christmas and New Year's Day I pee on a stick, and find myself secretly gratified by how the blue line hardens.

It is one of those seminal moments of womanhood. The pregnant moment. We have watched it on screen; we have read about it countless times, but when it becomes our own moment it's a fresh tale all of its own.

I quit smoking and settle to cooking with ear plugs up my nose. The smell of onions is unmanageable. Though I do not vomit it feels as though I'm rolling on a boat all day, the kind of rolling that makes people wish they would die.

Someone suggests that I have a state-of-the-art nuchal scan at a private clinic in Marylebone, an early diagnostic scan for Down's Syndrome. It is advice that I follow with the same acquiescence as the suggestion to apply oil in order to avoid stretch marks and drink ginger beer to avoid sickness. It is something I thoughtlessly do because another mother prescribes it. The test will put my mind at rest, she tells me.

I book it. Nothing has been at rest since the blue line.

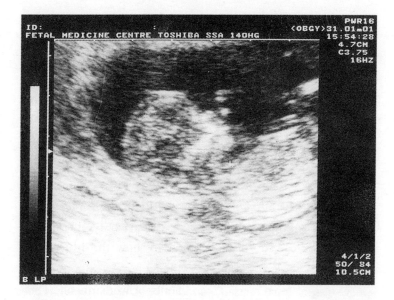

When we make the trip to London we find the waiting room on Wimpole Street is like a boutique hotel lobby. Reassuringly every other woman waiting is a good deal older than myself. One ashen-faced mother-to-be is slumped over in her chair.

Bloods are taken and we are called for a scan. I like scans. Coming face to face with the evidence of why I'm so sick is like having a recuperative sit-down on a long, unforgiving march. However, the upbeat conversation we are having with the sonographer about heartbeats and toe counting is beginning to dry up. When she takes the measurement of the foetus's neck a second time I hear her swallow. She measures again. Then she departs from the room and returns with someone more senior. Together they measure the neck a fourth time. No one says a word.

We are returned to the waiting room. The ashen-faced woman is still there.

Eventually we are called into a side room. Calculations have been made, a nurse tells us, using hormonal levels in the blood and nuchal translucency measurements, and the odds of a healthy baby have plummeted. The nurse gestures at her graph, pointing out that our foetus has fallen well outside the normal level. She looks me in the eye and says:

'We would recommend further tests.'

But this isn't what we paid for, I want to tell her. It really isn't.

Rather than eating a meal in Bloomsbury, as planned, we head straight for the train station. Our silence stretches the long way back into Cambridgeshire so that by the time we get home the blight is a good deal worse.

As night falls we receive more advice. It is from my father-in-law. He tells us we would be wasting our time with further tests. With these odds, as a doctor, he recommends that we immediately abort.

In film and in the novel, pregnancy and abortion are inextricably intertwined. Perhaps then it is inevitable that I find myself here, in a room that has the word 'counsellor' picked out on the door.

Boxed on the coffee table are tissues in salmon pink. Matthias, the consultant and the counsellor are talking of termination, without saying the word. The consultant wears a white coat, the counsellor a cardigan, and they pretend to include me in their 'we', but I am fixated with the tissues, and with the wrong.

Matt sits beside me, but I have never felt farther from him. The consultant and the counsellor kick around the edge of my silence. Though we have ignored my father-in-law, and this is not an abortion, it feels as though that is what will take place.

The risks of taking a sample of placenta tissue are high. Before the doctors can proceed they need to nail me down. The consultant hints that he won't go through with the invasive procedure unless we can reassure him that a negative result will precipitate a decision to terminate. It is not because he has a similar world view to Matthias's father, but because the procedure is so risky. If I want this baby, whatever the consequence, I am not sitting in the right place.

The counsellor breaks in, pulling her cardy hard over her bosom, hurrying to soften the statistics with more humane sums.

'It's a new test. We don't have enough experience to give you numbers.' The numbers she means are of how many babies have miscarried as a result of the procedure. 'In fact,' she pauses, 'in this hospital we have conducted this sampling technique only once.'

Matt reassures them. He has discussed it with his father. The test will not be wasted. If the foetus is unhealthy the right decision will be made.

In this moment I know there can be no right. No wrong. Only the responsibility for the decision being made. It is here, at my most lonely, that the mother in me unfurls, waking up to the silent story going on inside. The decision for how this tale ends can be no one else's but my own.

Lie 59: You'll be fine

Mum and Dad have told me to go back to sleep.

We, that is me and the newborn, have just escaped one of those first-world crises that deserves no sympathy at all – a loft conversion, the ceiling vomiting down the stairs. The plan is to stay with my parents in Ayr for the duration.

I lie there in the single bed I used infrequently as a teenager, staring at the cheap paper lampshade and the wobbly edge of paint between ceiling and wall. Through the curtained window, I can hear Dad's whistle as he pushes the buggy towards the beach.

This ground-floor bedroom is as serviceable as all the others I have inhabited. A room that had other functions in the months I was away. There is a bookcase filled with House Group reading material, and a collection of chairs pushed up against the walls for those mornings when the church group calls. Now the bed is crushed into a corner, so as to keep the baby from falling from it. I rearranged the furniture myself, like a maniac, the first night.

There is only the dry noise of the wind through the trees now Dad's whistle has died away. It is one of those rowdy sea winds that throws the branches against one another. Being in the midst of a strong wind is how it has felt since the morning the chorionic villus sampling results came in.

Within hours of receiving them, like a Victorian lady in crisis, I had a violent attack of the nerves.

My skin and my self crawled with something no scratch could soothe. I put it down to relief that our baby could live and guilt over how I had allowed myself to be coerced into believing only 'healthy' children deserve to.

My father-in-law, the doctor, who had advised us to abort, weighed in again, ringing with news that I had gone down with multiple sclerosis. 'The nerves' had left me weakened down one side of my body, pins and needles scattering through my limbs and my back.

When I mentioned the words 'multiple sclerosis' to the consultant at Addenbrooke's, his pencil snapped in half.

'MS employs the word *multiple* for a reason,' he said, his eyes fixed on my vast stomach, stowing the pencil halves in the drawer of his desk. 'No professional would diagnose you with it until you had had another deterioration. It would be no kindness to use that diagnosis at this stage.'

More than stupidly I then rang the MS Society for re-assurance, and was told that it was rare to have an 'episode' in pregnancy. 'The reason women are counselled not to have children', she said, 'is really about how quickly their symptoms deteriorate once a child is born. It is an exhausting time.'

And it is. Matthias has been back to work since we returned from hospital. When the midwife comes knocking and finds me alone, I confess to her that I don't know what the hell I am doing.

'Don't worry,' she tells me. 'If you've been parented well, you'll be fine.'

I take to my bed.

I am a terrible mother, and this knowing means I do not sleep, but lie rigid in my parents' single bed, staring at the paper lampshade in a curtained gloom.

Soon I am worrying whether Dad has bothered to take

the baby's hat and mittens with him, and once I struggle down from that worry the next one starts to loom. They have already been gone an hour. Worry has become a convincing cover for a yawning lack of love.

I have substituted milk. The Bean feeds until he's sick. He cries for hours. And each time he does I am unable to find the emotion to talk, or hug, or smile. Instead I lift my shirt with resignation, marooned on the sofa in front of some truly terrible daytime television, the constant pins and needles a ghostly reminder that self-catheterisation will be next.

I am not good at doing nothing either. Boredom has always felt dangerous. It is the time of day for a lynching, the time that leaves enough space for that appalling sickness for home. Made mute by the collective lies we tell ourselves about how wonderful new motherhood is, I have had no authentic conversation with anyone for months.

It will be the first time in my relationship with Mum that I am able to feel empathy for her, and what she might have gone through in those early years. It is hard enough having a single baby, without looking after two crazed stepchildren too. I try to imagine how she might have survived, and frankly can't.

While the building works at home slow to a standstill, away in Ayr I spend a good deal of time in church, or being pleasant to fellow congregation members in tedious community hall-type settings, elderly men peering down my shirt as I feed. But all of it is better than being alone with the knowledge of how terrible I am.

But Mum and Dad are good. Here the days are not as diabolical as they were at home. There the Bean was often

even more relieved than I when Matthias got in. They did baths together, they did crooning and they did love. In Scotland there is holding, and hugging too. Mum and Dad shuffle the Bean away at every opportunity so that they might sniff and tickle and poke. Each morning Dad walks along the seafront with dog and buggy. Back home, he sings. For whole hours our Bean forgets his hunger. He forgets to cry.

Through the curtained gloom I hear the dog's claws clack along the garden path outside and fly from the room. Head full of missing mittens, hats and feeds I find Dad out in the hall, bent over the buggy, lifting the Bean from beneath his blankets. He is singing in barely audible tones:

'If that mockingbird don't sing, Papa's going to buy . . .'

In the mouth of the hood the Bean's huge brown eyes blink in that sleepy slow way babies do, as if they want to check what's in front of them can't disappear. When his lids reopen the Bean watches love, transfixed.

Lie 60: Let me tell you a secret

Do I kid myself that by betraying my parents, I am telling the truth?

Truth to some is less important than privacy and I have violated theirs. It will be the biggest criticism laid against me – and I deserve it.

If we are weighing up the pros and cons of truth and privacy, in their marriage perhaps it was privacy that worked for Mum more. She had a secret, a secret that she and Dad shared. It gave them an opportunity to be intimate. It also gave her power, and it gave her control.

Secrets are a burden and a glee. They create insiders and outsiders. Secrets go hand in hand with prohibition, silence, furtiveness and intimacy. Not all secrets are lies. Our vote is our secret, and the discussions we have on juries as we reach a decision on guilt are too. In fact secrets are official government policy. Or can we argue that actually these are examples of privacy rather than secrecy? To keep things private is often motivated by a respect for our audience, as much as for ourselves. Our salary, our unsightly bare bottoms, the detail of the sex we had last night nobody else needs to know, or wants to. Whereas to keep a secret is to actively hide it – to stow the evidence, for example, of a terrible run of A-level results, directly in the bin.

Jung said that secrets act like a 'psychic poison'. They are literally unspeakable, and when told have a prohibitive price tag. We might speculate that secretive affairs enhance romantic relationships, but a paper in the *Journal of Social Psychology* found that, against the author's predictions, whether it is new love or old, furtive office fucks or long-standing double lives, secrets are a burden.

Infidelity or not, many relationships are heavy with secrets. We fall in love, not thinking it will be relevant in those early days to explain why sex in a particular position is not enjoyable, and then as things progress we grow less and less comfortable with admitting the truth. Dodgy finances, an STD, giving up a child for adoption can all become secrets. With the desire to avoid disapproval, often there are more secrets in a marriage than in any other kind of relationship. The honesty and openness that a husband and wife expect can force us to sometimes bury who we are.

Secrets exclude and this is probably why they are a regular feature of life in the playground. Liberating for a child, they are power. Sean likes secrets. When I told him that I thought Mum was illegitimate, he replied:

'Oh, I knew that, and she told me who he was.'

'So? Go on. Who?'

'I can't tell you.'

'What do you mean you can't tell me?' Even now remembering this conversation makes me furious. 'Of course you can tell me. She's dead.'

But he wouldn't.

The worst secrets are those we feel we cannot speak of to anyone. Often they are inextricably linked to shame. One school friend told me that she would wet the bed each night, only to have to return to her own mess every evening, without ever telling a soul. At school we had to keep our failings and our mess to ourselves; to be homesick was just as much a failing as peeing the bed. My sickness was the worst secret I've ever had to hold.

Until my father-in-law's 'multiple sclerosis' telephone diagnosis.

God, to have had more of a sense of humour. To have real-ised that he's an ignorant man, who doesn't like me at all.

But no. The pins and needles and its terror were a tale of misfortune I spoke of to no one. I said I was enjoying my new baby and I pretended I was thinking about anything other than MS.

Jung is right. This secret of mine was poison. I commit-ted myself totally to my symptoms with a self-absorption I still feel ashamed to admit to.

In worrying how I might be judged for the pathetic way I carry sickness I am not alone. When we become terminally ill, psychologists have found, we feel that we ought to be good. We are motivated to leave a good impression. It is the last chance we are given to do an important task well.

Although Mum and Dad must have felt angry at the un-fairness, terrified of what was to come, despairing over how little time there was left, neither admitted to these feelings. Always they were stoic and well behaved. In their dying they were heroic. This final secret of how difficult death is, they did not share.

Lie 61: We'll see you for your second course of chemotherapy in a month's time

The last time I ever spoke to Dad on the phone he was weeping. It was a cold November morning. Dark outside. In the distance I heard car doors slamming. The transportation had arrived to take him for chemotherapy. He could not walk the ten yards to the car. He had had the operation. And he had had the radiotherapy. This was the last ditch.

A glioblastoma multiforme is a hideous cancer in all respects. From one doctor's description of 'red and yellow', I imagined it suppurating with pus and blood. An image on Google shows what appears to be a brain with frostbite. It is blackened around the edges. Another shows sections where a tumour has dug in, seeping custard and raspberry. Wet.

The glioblastoma multiforme grade IV grows rapidly. It invades and alters neural function and, left untreated, is lethal. The silent areas of the brain allow tumours to become large before any symptoms arise. Prognosis is poor. The median survival for patients presenting with this type of cancer is about four months with surgery, and nine months when followed up with radiotherapy. One article remarks that prolonged treatment is futile and hospitalisation should be kept to a minimum.

After that final call I flew up to help collect him from hospital. I had my daughter with me, who was ten weeks old. We were accompanied by a family friend, as my mother could not bear to go.

Let us call the friend Susan.

In retrospect, as visiting companions go, she was not a good choice. Perhaps something had 'happened' between her and Dad. There had been a time when they went out together, presumably because she was attempting a Christian conversion. If this were the case wires would have inevitably got crossed. I'm guessing something embarrassing 'happened' because every time she invited the family round, Dad was militant and slept. Slept in any chair she waved him into, bolt upright, and almost as soon as he sat down.

As I lumbered down the Glasgow Western's windowed corridor I carried the baby in her car seat, shifting the weight from one arm to another. It was a long walk, the walls punctured by regular rectangles of safety glass. They offered views onto the wards either side. Elderly men, tucked in, ghosted each bed.

Behind me I could hear Susan struggle as she tried to keep up. She had been talking of death the length of the dual carriageway. Now there was only her breath and the rasp of her nylon tights.

Through the safety glass I searched for Dad's face.

We had passed the fourth door before I recognised him. He was the only man fully dressed and sitting up in a chair. He gazed through the exterior window at another building that cast a shadow across the room.

As we entered, the other patients, who were still tucked up, peered at us over the turn of their sheets. My father looked round with the smile of someone who was not sure who we were. Dumping the baby on his empty bed I kissed him, and for a moment he looked bewildered, his brow wrinkled with questions he was too afraid to ask.

I thought this latent confusion was because of the baby. He didn't think of me as a parent, but as a child. Yet it was to Susan that his eyes slid, tripping over the remains of the brain tumour and the hole it had left.

'You've got your hat on, Dad,' I said to ease the atmosphere. 'Everyone will think you're about to escape.'

His face relaxed. It was banter he was used to.

Susan busied herself with Dad's possessions, her backside protruding from his locker, putting things on the bed beside his bag. Her actions seemed dubious, and he reached for the small holdall.

'I'm just packing your bag, John,' she shouted.

The baby whined. A nurse, in white, appeared.

'What a wee one,' she said, stroking a cheek. 'Not often we get new babies like you in here.'

· The baby wriggled in her car seat and began that yawing cry that would soon become a roar. Relieved to have something to do, I slumped into a chair and hauled out a breast. All the men watched with frank curiosity as the baby's breathless whinging gave way to silence.

'Beautiful baby, Mr Doyle,' the nurse said. 'Is she your granddaughter?'

'Yes, John,' yelled Susan from the confines of the bedside locker. 'A new granddaughter.'

But he was more worried about his bag, clasping onto it tight. As the nurse took a turn with the rest of the patients, Susan pulled one edge of the bag towards her. She stuffed it with pyjamas, a tangerine and yesterday's newspaper. Dad's thin hand stretched to keep hold of the other end, exposing the hospital tag looped at his wrist.

As I continued to feed the baby another nurse arrived with a clipboard. She wore blue. My father shifted uncomfortably in his seat. He seemed to be dodging something at eye level that we could not see. The blue nurse looked from me, to my father, to Susan.

Even though Susan was slumped on the bed, wheezing from the packing exertion, she had an air of authority that we seemed to lack, for the blue nurse addressed her.

'Two pills before breakfast for the next four days.'

'Is everything all right, Dad?' I asked loudly, for I could see he didn't have his hearing aid in.

'Something's fallen,' he said.

'I can't see anything.' I tore the baby from my breast and placed her on the bed. 'Shall I have a look?'

'It's my hat. Can you see it?'

His hat was on his head, but I knelt down, nevertheless, to look where he was gesturing.

'There's nothing here,' I said from the floor. 'Maybe it was a tissue or something, because your hat is on your head.'

'Oh.'

The nurse in blue peered over her clipboard.

'Mr Doyle?' she said.

Dad looked up benignly.

'So we'll see you for your second course in a month's time.'

My father was now stooping, his hands waving above the floor as if to clutch at something. I placed my hand on his arm.

'Don't worry. You've still got your hat. What is it you're seeing?'

'Something dark,' he mumbled.

I picked up the baby and threw her against my shoulder. With a loud burp she emptied milk down my back.

'Where's Mum?' he asked.

'She's at home getting supper on.'

The nurse in white broke off her tour of the beds.

'Mr Doyle, you're not leaving us already?'

She held out her hands and I passed her the baby, the warm wetness of the milk on my shirt already turned cold.

'She's a wee doll, isn't she?' She leant down so my father could see my daughter's face. But Dad was trying to get up. He had heard the word 'leaving', and uttered by someone in uniform, it provoked action that my words – 'escape', 'car', 'home' – had not.

Yet co-ordination was impossible or he had not the strength for it. One hand was white as it clutched the arm of the chair from the exertion of trying to get to his feet. Each time he found a foothold on the smooth floor, he slumped down again, as if pushed. Susan bustled out to find a wheelchair.

'It's a long walk to the car,' I said to him. 'Better to get some wheels.'

Meanwhile the nurse walked the baby round from one patient to the next. I found it easier to watch her progress rather than make conversation with Dad. She sat down on the edge of one bed and the man's face lit up. His hand moved awkwardly out from beneath the coverlet. With extreme concentration he reached out his old, shaking fingers to stroke a curled and tiny fist.

Wheels located, the nurse dropped the baby into her car seat and together we braced ourselves against the bed to heave Dad into the wheelchair. He reached out for his bag.

Between the telephone conversation in the early darkness thirty-six hours before and the Glasgow Western, my father had slipped out of reach. Like a boat watched from shore.

I picked up the plastic bottle of pills. It was light. I had imagined intravenous torture, patients honking into buckets beside the bed. But this treatment appeared humane. I tucked the bottle in beside my daughter and belted her in.

Susan and I battled out of the hospital, carrying the car seat and hauling the wheelchair between us. The chair had all the effectiveness of a defective supermarket trolley. Dad clasped his bag on his lap.

When he squeezed into the hatchback it was with a horrible groan. Though he was now thin, he still filled the space, his hat pressed against the roof of the car, knees locked uncomfortably against the dashboard. He took a deep breath when we closed the door, as if he were having to make himself small, and asked again:

'Where's Mum?'

Lie 62: We agreed a story and she carried it off well

Mum has already moved on to the next stage of grief. With the jagged Westmorland slate embedded above Dad's grave she is packing up the house. I haven't moved on at all. I am still grieving the lie I need to believe in, my father as a trustworthy man. It is not hard. Mum has had the gravestone engraved with the ungrammatical epitaph 'Righter of Wrongs'.

Beneath his desk, boxes of possessions gather for the new house. On top there are Tupperware containers of floppy disks. I have agreed to go through each of Dad's computer files to see if there is anything to be kept. But I have no patience for his folders of archived letters and I eject disk after disk, throwing them towards the black bin liner at the centre of the room.

The trouble is that I can't stay focused. This morning my mother has told me she has burnt some 'incriminating evidence'. A photograph of Dad and a woman, both naked, and that bloody letter, found amongst his stamp collection, kept for the Italian stamp. It is the letter she mentioned a fortnight ago on a Norfolk campsite, a letter I've been trying to forget.

As I lob another disk into the rubbish I speculate again whether it is her imagination. I feel irritated that I have not seen the photograph, or the letter, for myself. My father, with his persistent undermining, has primed me. I never take Mum at her word.

When she heads out with the dog and the children I charge up to the attic. Perhaps I will find more sense of him up there. Wobbling from beam to beam over candyfloss insulation, I pass boxes and boxes of anger. Letters to the university where he last worked fill four crates alone.

I ignore the lever-arch binders, filled with correspondence, and begin to finger through a box which looks more chaotic. Loose sheets of paper and examination booklets lie disordered under an empty file. Here, amongst the weight of rage stretching beneath the eaves, are leaves of old fiction, scant diary entries and notes on an equation for enjoyment. I use his correspondence for 1999 as a seat and scan this last find. He cites enjoyment for a weekend as:

> *Eating Out;*
> *Bell Ringing;*
> *Swimming;*
> *Squash;*
> *Sex;*
> *Sightseeing.*

He has divided this list into two columns: FUN and MU-TUAL FUN. In the first column he notes '2 hours' for Pool. In the second he puts only '1'. So whilst he continued to swim or snooze or chat, my mother, I presume, grew restless on her lounge chair and wished to go. She did not get any fun out of the Squash, five of the seven hours they spent at the Beach, half of the meals they ate out and one of the two fifteen-minute periods they spent making love. He has converted his '100 Hours of Holiday' to percentages and concludes: 'Enjoyable (MUTUAL) – 12%; Enjoyable (SELF) – 7.5%'. To the remaining 80.5 per cent he gives a large question mark.

Up here amongst the Heriot-Watt exam notebooks and scraps of lined paper, I smell the grief of a relationship going sour. Of letters drafted and never sent, of words dying on his breath, emptied onto paper, feelings muted by the page.

I leaf through notes for stories that feature prophylactics and escape. Though it feels like letting myself slip some-where I do not want to go, I carry on reading.

Amongst some incomplete stories are four pages in red biro. Diary entries, Wednesday 13th to Thursday 21st. He is worrying away at a problem. The problem is not explicit and the players are parents of children I once knew. There is much discussion of arrangements, like teenagers planning the next few hours as though they are weeks. It is like a stirred pudding where six thirty-somethings are being slowly folded together until all the ingredients are mixed. On the final page, amongst talk of decanted home-brewed beer and uncooked chicken, he writes: 'We agreed a story that I'd been with Jan since 3.30 and she carried it off well.'

I trail over the sentences and paragraphs and think this must be fiction. This is not *him*. This is *not* him. This is not evidence either. Speaking of lying does not constitute sex.

I struggle down the ladder, the four sheets of foolscap flapping in my hand. I need confirmation. Jan, on her third or fourth husband, is impossible to trace. Much better to contact the German woman, Renata, using an Italian stamp. It will confirm or deny my mother's version. I feel the frenzy of a jilted lover, excited by thoughts of revenge. At the computer I Google her email address and fantastically it is there. I write to her, in a version of words, that I know of their affair. A lie to flush out the truth.

In the days before I receive her reply I read the four pages over and each time I get farther away from believing there is anything wrong – until Renata's answer arrives in my inbox. Though the woman is sorry for my 'distress', she writes, 'I am not penitent.' Their affair had lasted a year. Fiction coagulates to form fact. All the times he had berated my mother for Pestering and Interfering and Being Over The Top, she had been none of those things. She had smelt a rat. And he was it.

I go back to the red biro entry another time: 'We agreed a story that I'd been with Jan since 3.30 and she carried it off well.'

Here is the two-dimensional philanderer I never knew. In his own handwriting Dad shrinks to the pathetic cliché found in novels about lecturers, letcherers, who fuck their students and their colleagues' wives. A liar.

Or am I as flawed as he? These words of mine, the letters F – U – C – K all strung together omit the anticipation and the guilt. These feelings are the white space around the words. They are what is forgotten when the black lines are all that is left.

Lie 63: The testes are unremarkable

I make the decision that I must see what is left of my father. His brain lies in Glasgow's Southern General, donated to the team who work on glioblastoma multiforme. His was a tumour that wove insidiously through the folds of cortex above his left ear. It became enmeshed with his synapses, flowering like deceit.

Professor Greig, who cut his brain from its stem, has asked me to go straight up to the Neuropathology Department on the fifth floor.

The lift opens onto scarred double doors and a damp smell of wooden benches. Professor Greig gets up to shake my hand. In his office we sit down opposite one another, and I say:

'Where does it live?'

The question is out of me before I can think of something more sensible to ask.

Professor Greig rises from his chair and walks across the corridor to another room. He returns with a shallow empty bucket in white.

'We store our donations in these.'

The consistency of the brain is like jelly, he tells me, and very difficult to work with. And it was in a larger bucket that the material, as he calls it, was 'fixed'. Once the wet tissue was hard, what was left of my father was cut into fourteen pieces.

He leans over and points out a book lying open next to me on the desk.

I look. The photograph is black and white, and shows a full brain sliced and arranged, left to right. Perhaps, I think, it will be less gruesome to view in pieces than as a bulk of creases and folds, recognisable as a brain. And as something that was once his. In my anxiety at what must come I tear on, saying:

'I wondered why his testes were not examined in the autopsy. I wondered whether it was a kind of man-to-man thing, that you left this part of him alone as a mark of respect.'

Professor Greig looks at me blankly.

This fact has been bugging me for at least a week. Another pathologist will later explain that the testes might have been omitted from a full autopsy because they're a bit of a 'faff'. Usually they need to be poked up into the stomach cavity, and if tissue is 'retained', or 'lost', a golf ball is thought to make a decent replacement.

I repeat the question.

'The post-mortem report states that the testes were not examined.'

Professor Greig rises, and it is the only moment that afternoon when he looks flustered, reaching over his desk for the post-mortem report. Carefully he turns the page and apologises. It is an oversight, he says, asking if I am worried that the cancer had spread.

'No, I am not worried about the cancer,' I tell him. 'It was only that it seemed a glaring omission.'

'Excuse me?'

Professor Greig has the look of someone in the audience of Wagner's Ring Cycle who's neglected to read the plot synopsis. I say how my father was unfaithful to my mother the whole of their married lives. And what has infuriated me the most, and is so bloody typical, is how his testes have defied that damning autopsy label which defined each of his other organs – 'unremarkable'.

'Will I be able to take it home?' I ask a bewildered Professor Greig.

'The donation?'

'I was thinking of a sea burial.' The Ireland question had come up a number of times. Turfing his remains into the Irish Sea from a ferry feels appropriate.

Professor Greig tells me that there is a daunting amount of paperwork just for it to leave the building, and I would have to be prepared to dig a six-foot hole. Brains have the consistency of Semtex, he says:

'You wouldn't get it past security.'

Closing the book he tells me that the viewing of the remains has been arranged downstairs in the mortuary chapel. In the lift, once the doors have concertinaed closed, he says cheerily to another doctor:

'This young lady has come to discuss a donation her family have made to the department.'

The man colours and the exchange gives me the feeling that in all his years as a pathologist, and he is due for retirement in a month, Professor Greig has never experienced a mission like this.

At the mortuary we ring the bell. A shadow hobbles into view. Mr Stewart, the mortician, has a stick. Professor Greig tells me that Mr Stewart has hurt his back and Mr Stewart, in white coat and blue scrubs, nods.

We enter the chapel, and again Professor Greig tells me that I may not want to see it. But there is nothing that would make me turn back now.

Mr Stewart opens the door to the viewing chamber. There is a small room: no chairs, a glass panel in one wall. The window is curtained. Behind it appears a hospital trolley-bed pushed up beneath the glass. Covered in white linen, it carries the brain.

The sections are placed in three rows on a white tray. Dad's label is soaked and almost unreadable with its autopsy name, number and place of death: 'Doyle AO30139: Ayrshire Hospice'.

The grey and white matter are in two diabolical shades of beige, the fan of nerve endings clear as the roots of a tree. The slices increase in size from the prefrontal section through to the diced gristle of the brain stem. The seventh slice has a small hole, the eighth an even larger one, whilst

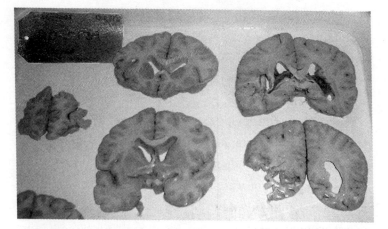

the ninth and tenth show ragged edges. The cavity is enormous.

The men wait for me to speak. It is impossible to imagine that this is him. This, in some essential way, is who Dad was, and who he pretended he wasn't.

I start to ask questions about the cavity and the discoloration, but I no longer care what the answers are.

I realise I should emulate Professor Greig. As part of his 'unremarkable' autopsy he has retained sections of healthy tissue to store alongside what was diseased. He has remained impartial in the face of a rampant brain tumour.

He has accepted my father as he was.

Lie 64: I am good

There are, according to critics, good memoirs and bad ones. Bad ones make their authors, like 'professional victim' Dave

Pelzer, hundreds of thousands of dollars. *A Child Called It* remained on the bestseller list for 448 weeks. What is bad is sentimentality and sensational over-indulgence. No memoirist, either (especially if they're earning tons of money), should be bitter.

Those who write about themselves fall into two camps: sadists and masochists, and it is the sadists, we must presume, who are bad. They ruin literature.

This is a genre for which forgiveness is a highly valued, and a rare commodity. One book chapter on the ethics of misery memoir asks: what are we to do with autobiographers who cannot forgive their parents?

Why should we do anything? Just because these writers cannot forgive, does that really make what they have to say bad? Dave Pelzer's inability to empathise with his abuser may not be a choice. Neglect literally reduces brain volume. Synaptic pruning, a process which begins in the first one to two years of life, crops axons, dendrites and synapses that have been underused in early childhood. For these children it means shaving love short. Perhaps, rather than being bad, these memoirs are the most honest version of self that they can be, and the most 'true'.

Am I bad? Even by asking the question, do I haul myself away from giving a truthful account? Or simply reveal myself as desperate to be liked and worried what everyone else thinks? Because I have worried about being good. Being good is often on my mind. I guess in this regard, though, I am bad – I have admitted that I am still struggling to forgive, and even if I haven't admitted it, my underlying tone will have given me away.

More than forgiveness, it is betrayal that many of those who find themselves subjects of memoir would say is unethical. Being understood comes a distant second when judged against loyalty. These things I have written are private, and the secrets I have told are not mine. In fact loyalty to the Doyles ranks greater than almost anything else. Just as it feels like subjugation to remain dutiful to someone else's secrets, it is also oppressive when parents and siblings are forced to play a role in a tale they did not write. My brothers may feel as though I've hauled them on stage and forced them to speak a series of terrible lines.

I did ask some of my characters (not Adrian, or Sean yet) if they would like a right to reply, but Violet and Ed declined. Perhaps it is more satisfying to feel justifiably pissed off.

Which they will be. The reaction to Karl Ove Knausgaard's autobiographical *My Struggle* has included hate mail, death threats and lawsuits. The 'K' section of a bookshop was torched. In the *Paris Review* Knausgaard excuses himself: 'I was so frustrated that I did not foresee the consequences . . . There was a certain desperation that made it possible.' Ignorance is not an excuse I can claim. I have foreseen the consequences, and this must make me look worse. I am rather hoping that, as many of my family are not readers, they won't notice that this has happened.

Which relies heavily on the extremely generous note that Mum wrote once she was no longer able to speak – 'Miranda, you have my full permission to write anything you want.' She, more than anyone else, would want me to forgive.

Yet we are only capable of forgiveness when we fully understand one another. Something I am struggling with. The monumental levels of deceit make it difficult to fathom any truths about my parents' marriage, their motivations, their selves. I will have left out thoughts, ideas, feelings that were enormously important to them. All I can hope is that what I can't see – my own ignorance about them and about myself – you can, because it is in this space between me and you, writer and reader, that memoir finds its voice.

Lie 65: It was just a joke

Months have passed since the Italian stamp debacle and here we are, me and the children, marking out the long weeks of holiday 'at Granny's'. The beach and her love of the children alleviate the resentment of having to visit this tired seaside town that has never been home to me.

My mother has moved to granny-friendly accommodation, and is surrounded by neighbours who are older and more decrepit. Although she is only sixty she talks of converting the bath to a shower, of the convenience of having her bedroom downstairs. Tension plays out over the fact I am holidaying at hers rather than she with us. She freely admits that she would prefer not cooking for us at all.

But irritation over the cooking is camouflage for something much more grave. The lie is still amongst us. We trip over it wherever we step.

Day three I find Mum seated in Dad's ugly recliner, attempting nonchalance. Yanking on the handle she tips it back, so the footrest kicks up her striped socked feet. There is a hole, which she points out to the two-year-old.

'Look, Granny's got a hole in her sock.' The toddler toddles over to inspect. The big toe wiggles. Mum reaches over and pulls out some white paper and a red felt-tip and says: 'Go on and draw Granny a huge red hippopotamus?' Then calls through to the five-year-old, crouched over a train set in the other room: 'When you've got the track finished I'll come through and see it.'

I wonder whether she was always this good at mothering, or if it is only mothering me that is so hard. I struggle so with it myself.

Both children now distracted, she pulls the striped polycotton back over her toe.

'We must not tell the boys.'

'The boys?'

She must mean my brothers, but it is far too late for that. I have told everyone.

'I mean,' she says, 'if they ask, of course, you can tell them. But only if they ask.'

Which makes this another Catholic lie, where by not speaking the truth the hope is that it will just wither away, a technique she must have picked up from Dad. It is not an observation I make aloud. Partly because I have not admitted to the illicit emails or furtive checks of her address book for all the women Dad might have shagged.

She shuffles forward on the recliner and says calmly:

'It's not something they need to know.'

A catalogue of knowing, which she must already regret.

'So you didn't know yourself?' I say. 'You didn't know until the Italian stamp?'

She looks at me blandly.

'This is the first you knew?' I repeat, meaning generally – that Dad had affairs.

'Yes,' she says, getting up to swoop the toddler and her hippopotamus scrawl away from the dog.

Her 'yes' is not a lie. It relates, I will later realise, only to the specific case of the German, Renata, rather than his promiscuity in general.

'Look,' she calls over her shoulder, 'I've only got pasta. Shall we do that for tea?'

As she trails the dog and toddler through to the finished train track, I am struck by her ignorance – how could she have not known, I wonder, without giving my own idiocy any thought.

It is not a point I am able to make. Within hours of this dubious exchange, my mother is gratefully diverted by something much more important. Lunging for a ball the dog breaks (not fatally) his back. And it is in this final frazzled week that the email arrives. In the past, when she could get to them before me, my mother read my postcards. The Outlook email programme that I have left open on her desktop screen proves to be the contemporary equivalent. It is not that she must open the email to see it, but rather, like the postcard, it advertises its content, and she barrels out of her office as if she's been struck.

It's not even an email from a friend. It's an email from another mother.

I have said diabolical things about mine before to friends and acquaintances. She was a source of much of my bleak comedy.

The first sentence of Caroline's email reads: 'Have you strangled your mother yet?'

'It was a joke,' I tell Mum, fear burning black within me. 'Most daughters make jokes about their mothers.'

And they do, but our relationship is no joke. Too much is broken. However, I know I am on safe ground. Both of us remember, as we stand there in the hall, that she spent much of her twenties and thirties whining about her own mother too.

Perhaps it is this irony, or seeing the lie of our relationship laid bare, or just the sense of betrayal that the question provoked, but whatever it is Mum does not speak the rest of the afternoon and goes to bed early without a word.

As Caroline predicted, Mum will be strangled slowly.

Within a year she is dead. It is as though this email kills her. That very night her diseased motor neurones begin the inexorable process of giving up her ghost.

Lie 66: Jesus loves me

Though Mum's nervous system was already beginning to let her down, all she noticed at first was the slur. Maybe I noticed it too, but couldn't bring myself to say. You see, I had well and truly had it with guilt. In the bitter weeks after she asked me not to tell the 'boys', I began digging for skeletons. The first was school. From what I've recorded in my diary her answers were blithe:

'I never thought Aberlour was right for you. Or Gordonstoun for that matter.'

Then the dog would need something, or she'd be rescued by a House Group call. Sometimes, when there was no available distraction, she'd go on the offensive.

'Sending you away to school gave *me* a nervous breakdown!'

Thwarted, I turned my energy to Dad, taking a different tack. I was sorry, I told her, for all the times I had trusted him over her.

However, even when I was the one apologising the subject still changed. Like dogs and bones I was frustrated enough to shout:

'It's not for you to feel humiliated or guilty. No man, under the same circumstances, would blame himself.'

'Why can't you just be grateful that your children had the kind of grandfather they did?' She burst into tears. 'And why isn't Matthias here?'

It was then that I realised, as far as she was concerned, my husband and children were amongst the few things I had got right. The marriage story was the one I clung to, because for Mum I was nothing without it. I wish knowing these things had happened after her death, rather than in the months of her dying, but epiphanies are hard to plan. Sick, but still undiagnosed, she called first thing one morning, weeping.

'I can't trust you any more,' she blurted. 'Not at all.'

Months later, after she had lost the capacity for speech, Sean asked her whether she and I got on. She replied in blue biro: 'off + on'.

Without knowing how ill she was I withdrew from the daily phone call and regular visits, reassuring myself that at least there was still the dog and still Jesus. Although, in those last months, when her toes had curled and her voice had silenced, maybe she wondered if He, like us, had forsaken her. Or perhaps she kidded herself that whatever hellish journey she was on, it was nonstop and direct, with a destination plate that picked out in capitals the word 'HEAVEN'.

But how could she really have held on to that story? In the final few weeks of her life her despair was palpable, the illness cruel. Jesus was like a log in a fast-moving river. He kept slipping from her grasp as she was dragged downstream, the rest of us, hands in our pockets, watching from shore.

Lie 67: No it wasn't misgusting

Within a few weeks of the strangle email, apart from the slurring Mum is psychologically up and down, or as doctors call it, emotionally incontinent. It is September. She is put on antidepressants. I have depressed her for sure.

A long history of her psychological lows proves to be a diagnostic handicap. The professional presumption is that her symptoms are psychosomatic. Although she already has debilitating physical changes to report at her first appointment on 30 August, it is not until February the following year that she is diagnosed. Her diary is painful to read. By Christmas she is being helped to the car, and into her seatbelt. Every day she feels 'shattered'. She cries uncontrollably, she is very 'wobbly' on her feet, finds her voice 'very ropey' and suffers long and intense dizzy spells. Dr Bowman tells her on 11 January: 'These drugs [meaning her antidepressants] all have side effects. It will be interesting to see.'

'Again I felt really angry,' she writes, 'no real taking on board that I have become totally incapacitated by taking this drug.'

She hopes that the GP will take her seriously. It will be a hope that is answered in the bleakest terms.

In the meantime the slurring gets worse. Then her balance. She falls over. I am speaking to her every day, and then I begin to withdraw. My mother's need has grown so overwhelming that I spinelessly go along with the doctor's diagnosis of clinical despair.

Her counsellor suggests that she email her children and

ask us to outline the reasons why she is a great mother. I hesitate to tell you my response. Rather than risk putting anything down in writing I call. Not that I say so explicitly, but in that moment I can think of absolutely nothing that is great about her mothering. Perhaps I bully her, asking her what on earth it is that she wants me to say. Can't she see that she's forcing us to tell her only what she wants to hear? This conversation I will come to regret. To have lied would have been a much more gracious response than the truth.

Finally diagnosed with amyotrophic lateral sclerosis (ALS) or, more simply, motor neurone disease in February, her first and fleeting reaction is relief.

When I see her at home in March 2006, my diary reads: 'Last day. Matthias cuts her toe nails, thick as hooves. We uncurl her shoulder support, tangled beneath her bra. We push and cook and clean and rearrange and all the while I am thinking – do I have the energy for this again? This dying that needs to be done.'

After her death a GP tells me that doctors refer to a book of illnesses as a guide in professional practice. It is a book bigger and deeper than a well, and of all those ailments, chronic or acute, that are named between its covers it is motor neurone disease, she says, that every clinician wishes never to have to confront.

It strangled Mum slowly, yet burned along her neuro-muscular pathways like fire through grass. Within a couple of months a feeding tube was attached to her stomach and she was issued with a speaking machine, an electric wheel-chair and someone to take her to the toilet at night. Quite literally her toes curled up. The last weeks of her life were spent in a hospice, three doors down from where Dad had died. She struggled to breathe.

Last time, with Dad, we had experienced the dying days together. Like pensioners waiting at a bus stop, we would sit in companionable silence at bedsides and outside consulting rooms. Though Dad spoke to other visitors he slowly stopped speaking to us, either because he did not think us worth pretending to, or because he trusted us enough not to have to.

At her bedside that August I faced a lonely truth. She had slipped from visitor to patient and without her beside me through her own dying days, I had no courage. I longed for her struggle to be over, selfishly hoping for my own to be over too.

'They have tanked her up with sedative like an elephant so she'll sleep, her face fallen in a great sag of despair.' I had not brought those who were easier to love with me. Matthias, and our children, I left at home. It was a final disappointment that I hope she was able to forgive.

When others said their goodbyes an eye would open, large and swimming. One by one she watched them go until only Ed and I remained. Together we counted between each breath and got as far as seventeen. 'Sometimes we two look up from our writing and Sudoku to wait in the silence for her gasp.'

Both desperate to dive into the car and run. She breathed on.

'I said goodbye tonight and again those brown, misted irises glimmered. Her hand fluttered a wave and I wept. Have wept a good part of the day.'

By dawn she was making horrible sounds. Ed retreated

to the family room as the rattle deteriorated to a groan. Then a 'sickeningly wet gurgle'.

'They have lain her on her back so as to quicken the pace, her face the colour of a stormy sky. Her breath stops – twenty elephants. Twenty-five, mucus bubbles from her mouth. The hospital chaplain says a prayer as the snotty bubbles grow and fall, trailing green tears on her cheek.'

Apparently I attempt to wipe the slurp from her chin with a tissue, and yet it seeps and runs, a pool gathered in the well of her mouth. With the sticky tissue still in my hand I back from the room, jogging towards the family area. The curtains are open, a clean summer morning visible through the window. Ed is at his computer. Distracted he looks up.

'She's dead,' I tell him and pass into the bathroom.

I wash my hands a long time. When I reappear I find him ready and packed to go. Through the fire door we watch her body being wheeled away. Then with our bags over our shoulders we jog back to the ward, ripping everything from the notice board by her bed, emptying her cupboard into plastic bags. Within twenty minutes we are in the car, the relief so tangible it feels like that bus scene in the closing minutes of *The Graduate*. We say nothing.

On the way out of town we stop at the same funeral director's that had buried Dad. Remaining on our feet we deal with catering, floral tributes and the cemetery paperwork, and when the undertaker pulls out the coffin catalogue we respond in unison:

'Same again.'

Two days later my daughter asks:

'Was it misgusting when Granny died?'

My diary claims that as I try to divert her with talk of nighties and pyjamas, she blurts:

'Tell me the truth.'

Lie 68: Stickers are fair

'So how'll we carve up the stuff?' asked Adrian.

Someone suggested stickers.

Stickers will be the last game that my three brothers and I ever sit down together to play. There were a few in the art cupboard my mother had established for visiting children, and the refugees at Dungavel House Removal Centre, where she volunteered.

Adrian began to sticker the items he wanted.

'Anyone else interested?' he asked, his circle of green already pressed in place.

Ed took up a couple of stickers of his own. Sean and I left the room. We didn't want to play.

The next morning we buried Mum, and everyone headed south.

Though stickerless and the only one with young children, a few weeks later it fell to me to pack the house. I suppose I was the girl. It took me two weekends. There was too much to manage in one. Sean, also stickerless, turned up both times. The first weekend, I arrived a day earlier so as to get as much packed as I could before Sean arrived. A firefighter, he always takes an emergency approach.

I worked through Mum's stuff, packing, sorting. Then I

lay awake most of the night, every single light in the house on. By the time Sean arrived the following morning, I had emptied the sitting room, two bedrooms and the bathroom, arranging her possessions into a charity pile, a sticker pile and rubbish.

As soon as he was through the door, he tore through it all. Everything, bar the stickered furniture, was slung into the back of the car for the hospice shop, including the rubbish. As he left, he went through each of her coat pockets in the porch and then took off.

Back from the hospice shop he trailed me.

'What do you want me to do?'

I asked him to pack away some paper trays and boxes from the study.

'But they make the place look homey.'

'Okay. What about the shells in the conservatory? Put them in the bin?'

Same response.

'The only thing left then, Sean, is the kitchen.'

'I'll go have a look at the garage.'

When I went out to see what he'd achieved half an hour later, he and his car were gone. My diary entry from the return flight reads: 'Feel too exhausted and terrorised to give any of this the vocabulary it deserves.'

The second weekend there was fog at Stansted and I was late. Sean was already in town, but not in the house. I had only two hours till the Pickford's van arrived to collect Adrian's furniture, and I still had the kitchen to do.

An uncle and aunt, on Dad's side, arrived on my tail.

'Good-quality stuff,' Uncle Richard said to himself on

his way out to the garage. 'Good-quality stuff.'

Three dear women from church arrived soon after and rolled up their sleeves. I had never been so grateful to see anyone.

Uncle Richard peered over our shoulders as we packed. Saucepans, plant pots, telephone, lamps, he disappeared. At one point I saw him with a windbreak under one arm and a brass coffee pot under the other, heading out to the car. The Ford Focus wallowed low on its axles. A little while later, he was seen trying to manhandle a large pine box into the boot. It wouldn't fit.

'You cannae leave that to the hospice,' he shouted over his shoulder, parking the box on the verge amongst the stickers. 'Take it yourself.'

Too exhausted to argue, I left it where it was.

By five the house was empty, the Pickford's van loaded and the rellies headed east. I stood in the derelict house, feeling as though I'd been raped.

As I waited in the airport terminal, I sent a text to Adrian, who was receiving the Pickford's delivery.

'There's an extra piece of furniture in the shipment,' I told him. 'I'll come pick it up when I can.'

'Really?' he pinged back. 'My sticker must have fallen off it. Unless you are really desperate I was rather looking forward to owning the chest myself.'

'I'm not "really desperate" but thank you.'

'Well then,' he replied, 'I look forward to receiving your cheque for £41.62 in carriage.'

Perhaps he is hard-wired to escalate. Escalation is, I have later learned, essential if you want to win.

But I was done with losing. I emailed Adrian a bill for the cost of my flights north.

'I have donated the trunk to Oxfam,' he replied.

'All items of furniture are still in the possession of the executors. You have no right to get rid of anything without the full consent of every beneficiary,' I lied. 'I have contacted my lawyer.'

His final email was apoplectic.

'You are insulting,' he wrote, 'and bullying and I never ever want to see you again.'

I picked up the chest a fortnight later, on our way south to Brighton. Forlornly it sat on another verge. Put out.

Lie 69: It's not easy for me to do this

I don't remember Dad ever saying to Mum that fundamental sentence – the one using those all-important pronouns, 'I' and 'you', with which to sandwich love. But that is no proof that he didn't say it.

Of sorrys – the other indispensable currency of any successful relationship – he never spoke.

I am reminded of the ghastly apology dilemma when, out of the blue, I receive a letter from Adrian. We haven't spoken in a decade, and the first word out of my mouth, as I look at the signature, is an expletive. He is the last person on earth I want a sorry from.

Thankfully though, it is not true remorse. He writes, by hand: 'it is not in my nature to back down or give in.'

The only relief, I tell myself, is that a sorry on these terms needs no forgiveness at all.

When I was younger not saying sorry was something that enraged my mother. Understandably. Perhaps Dad never said he was sorry, because he wasn't. Sleeping with other women was not something he could ever feel sorry about.

Later the lack of apology became a family joke. We would tease him with it, and he'd giggle, but still he would never allow the incriminating word to pass his lips.

A paper in the *European Journal of Social Psychology* outlines that although apologies do make apologisers feel good, refusing to say sorry makes withholders feel even better. Empowered, and in more control, they ironically have a boosted sense of integrity when asked to relate the experience.

Narcissists, to avoid an apology, prefer diversionary tactics – they will tend to give a present rather than apologise,

or will bury the S-word in a self-justificatory lecture. Or worse, indulge in self-berating, so as to compete with the victim over who feels worse.

The *Encyclopaedia of Deception*'s entry on 'Infidelity' notes that if philandering doesn't kill a relationship it will be because the deceived party has either colluded or connived.

So Mum found a way of getting round the lack of apology – with the reusable sorry card. Dad would only have to sign and date it, in order to show that his repentance was current, then leave it on her desk.

After Mum's death, I found proof that she had always been complicit. To me it was evidence that the reason our own relationship had suffered was not that she had gone along with his philandering, but that she had pretended to me that she hadn't.

The dishonesty that lurched between us, in retrospect, had robbed our relationship of authenticity. She had often begged me to be honest with her, and I had. Most of the time. Unlike my father, I had never wanted her to be anything other than who she was, imagining that whatever conversation we were having, though flawed, was sincere.

Under her bed, their bed, I found the reusable sorry card, the envelope a catalogue of apologies.

'John:' in blue felt-tip – 'The re-usable card!' Beneath is her '+ again' in black biro, '& back', in Dad's handwriting, 'definitely' (misspelled) in hers, and then 'July – Maureen, in pencil in case we run out of space. I'm the one on the right!' Two more dates follow, both in her hand.

On the cover there is a blushing cartoon mouse with the words: 'I'm remorseful, regretful, repentant, contrite, humbled, grief-stricken, self-accusing, eating humble pie . . . Well let's face it . . .' and then inside the card '. . . I'm really very sorry.' Other than these card manufacturer's words, it is completely blank.

There is also a pile of Valentine cards, a haul of sentimentality and sweetness I never anticipated. One pictures two birds:

'Do you love me?' says the first.

'Of course I do.'

'Say it then.'

'I love you.'

'Say it with feeling.'

'I luuurve you.'

'LOUDER.'

'I love you, I love you, I love you, I love you!'

There is a gap, the bird who has just spoken awash with sweat. The other whispers:

'Promise?'

Again, though there are no words inside the card, it passes back and forth between them till finally there is a single entry from 2002, the year Dad died. It is in his handwriting, the letters already crooked with cancer: 'Thanks for all you've done.'

Finally, wedged beneath the cards, in a plastic wallet, is a full sermon, typed up. Delivered in the nineties by Dad alone at pulpits across Scotland, it spread the good news on marriage. Each Sunday he told the congregation that he had realised 'how impossible it would be to live without each other'.

Lie 70: Always tell the truth

'I' is a fragile mark. Apart from the indefinite article 'a', which must always be bolstered by a noun, 'I' is the shortest word in the English language. Though it looks thin and insubstantial, our 'I' feels huge. Capitalised, when 'me', 'he' and 'she' are not, it has a whine, even on the page, like a screaming gull.

The psychologist Robert Kurzban argues that this single line, this shortest word, is a lie. We have no unitary self, because our minds are modular, with distinct biological processes and functional specialisations which are necessarily isolated from one another. Like a governmental institution where departments jealously guard information from each other, the mind is not designed to maximise accuracy. Truth falls between the cracks.

Although 'representing things that are true is . . . useful',
such as the speed a car is travelling as we step off the kerb,
or that a fire is hot, our brains in a social setting are less
motivated to be accurate and therefore honest.

However, our conscious selves do feel motivated. Amongst
the most prized qualities of being human, researchers at the
University of London found, was honesty. In another study,
researchers asked volunteers to lie in order to gain money;
although they were speaking to strangers, most chose to tell
the truth until the financial loss tipped over the $20 thresh-
old. Many studies corroborate these findings. Humans are
prepared to sacrifice economic payoffs in the interest of
being honest. We weigh up the benefits of integrity with the
benefits of self-interest, and lying to those we are intimate
with, for many of us, is just too high a price to pay.

Lies are constructed while truths are retrieved, which
leaves a lie at a disadvantage. The brain is motivated to
privilege the less costly option. Truthfulness.

Perhaps then we can blame cognitive load, the mental
fatigue of lying, for my mother's deterioration into truth
(although she would probably tell you that it was Jesus).
However, what she cannot have noticed is that to embark
on truth-telling in the midst of a lie is the most exhausting
thing of all. Especially once she realised that she'd made a
mistake and didn't want to tell it at all.

Amongst liars the most common U-turn is when an adulterer wants to make a clean breast of things. Many argue
that they are motivated by self-interest. Discomfited by
shame and guilt they tell the truth to make themselves feel
better, and inevitably make the wronged party feel a good

deal worse. Mira Kirshenbaum, author of *When Good People Have Affairs*, is adamant that an adulterer must never confess, even when asked directly. The choice, as she sees it, is not between good and bad, but between honesty and hurt. Avoiding hurt is always a better moral choice, she argues, than disclosure.

My mother maybe did not imagine that her honesty would be hurtful. However, to me it feels like an attack on my self. Many of the memories I had stacked up in the past became, in the face of her truths, a lie. We define ourselves through memory, and if we cannot rely upon our memories, we feel betrayed.

Is it fair to claim, though, that Mum has trashed my memories? I have more likely trashed them myself. When I check my diaries, my memory has been selective. Mum had tried to embark on some truth-telling before. One entry for December 1983, when I was fifteen, reads: 'My mother thinks Dad's having an affair with someone we met in Corfu.'

But at fifteen there were other, more pressing things on my mind. Like how to survive another three years at boarding school. This news provoked only the tired question: why is she telling me? Sitting thousands of miles away from her in Scotland it was information I could do nothing with. I 'forgot'.

Or did Kurzban's modular mind – this fractured 'I' of mine – out of a sense of inconvenience, compartmentalise and bury? He suggests that the cognitive subsystems that make up our brain are like a 'Machiavellian spin doctor'. Not sure how the major decisions have been made, the self is like a press secretary with access to limited information that uncomfortably must be explained. We are most at risk of self-deception when we need to explain ourselves. Deceit creeps in through the back door.

So I must apologise. Faced with unreliable memories, self-deceit, some lies and Kurzban's fractured, out-of-touch self, this narrative, at best, can be only a thin imitation of how things were. In fact someone who features in these stories laughed when she read them:

'That was not how it was, or how you were.'

Lie 71: I'd just have to kill some people

What is the penultimate lie? Let's give this one to Sean.

It's a cliffhanger.

He arrives straight off a night shift at Heathrow. We go out for lunch, just the two of us, and though Dad's been dead more than a decade, we talk about him. With the two of us he's a popular subject. Something on which we can both agree. I always concede that for Sean it was worse.

Maybe we talk about Adrian too. We definitely talk about Ed. We are always nice about Ed.

Then we make the obligatory trip to Costa. Sean likes Costa. A lot.

Back home, waiting for the children to get in from school, through the window we see a squirrel digging up the beds. We watch in silence as it begins to tackle the lawn.

'I've got a squirrel trap at home,' Sean says eventually. 'They love peanut butter.'

We continue to watch as another dodges between the struts in the fence.

'Does the trap kill them?'

'Nah,' he says. 'I drop them by my mate's, in the flat below, and he takes them out with an air rifle.' He continues to stare into the garden. 'I don't like doing it myself.'

At the front of the house we hear my twelve-year-old trailing bags and an indifferent day in with her. Soon the fifteen-year-old tramps home too. He acknowledges us with a nod, and automatically empties the biscuit drawer.

Not waiting for him to start eating, Sean is already on his feet, like a boxer dancing in his corner. Pretending he wants to show the teenager some martial arts moves, he swiftly puts him in a headlock on the kitchen floor, shouting:

'What are you going to do now? You're immobilised. Look,' he pulls the arm tighter. 'I can do anything.'

A wooden spoon is broken in the melee, and something crashes to the floor.

Finally the teenager struggles back to his feet, and Sean bounds back to the table.

'From my flat, on a Tuesday,' he says, 'you can hear the alarm test at Broadmoor. I keep thinking, you know, that would be the way to live. No rent, no worries, my own little cell. I'd just have to kill some people.' The twelve-year-old has got a look on her face that mirrors how I feel. 'More than ten would probably do it and I've got a list.' He looks at me. 'Adrian's at the top, but don't worry, Mir, they'd probably catch me before I got to you. You're a bit further down.'

Lie 72: With my body I thee worship

I'm a week late delivering my manuscript. It's a common complaint made about writers. Rather than get on with it, we do the laundry, masturbate, or pretend to be interested in the conversation we have struck up in the Asda queue.

I need distraction. Only yesterday I told Ed and Sean what I was writing, and I've had a stomach ache ever since.

So as we reach the inevitable final days, deadline looming, you find me here, in a cramped downstairs lavatory raking through shells. Small scavenged seashells in a dish, housed beside the toilet paper. I think the shells were originally Mum's, slung together with some scented granules to form a homemade odoriser – a kind of shell pot pourri – and I'm wondering whether I should just bin them. Do they smell good any more, or are they just collecting dust? Toilets cleaned, floor wiped, I am resorting to anything to take my mind off my stomach and what I have written.

Continuing to stir, I wonder if there is any way that I could make everything smell better. My fingers clattering through cockle and whelk, something catches the light.

It is not a shell.

I back out of the lav, the dish at arm's length.

It is the kind of moment that whispers of faeries, but I am thinking only of gremlins.

What is not shell is gold. A slim circle of it. A finger-sized circle. I sit down and squint at the letters spiralling within. Unreadable.

Or is that an eternity symbol?

If this is Mum's wedding ring (and it better not be), why isn't it in her coffin with her? No one would have removed it from her. I would have had it buried with her, had anyone asked.

But if it is her ring, why didn't any of us notice that she'd ditched it? Or had the motor neurone disease shrunk her so fast, so small that she worried it might get lost? Taking it off was a way of keeping it safe. But then why toss it amongst seashells, stowed on a windowsill that she would not have been able to reach in her wheelchair?

Shells that I had asked Sean to throw out the weekend we emptied the house. Which must be why they've ended up with me, too guilty to throw them myself.

I look at the ring again.

What was said when it was slid over knuckle and skin the first time? Were bodies to be honoured? Cherished? Was there talk of faithfulness, fidelity and forsaking all others?

When my daughter appears asking: 'When's lunch?' I am still sitting where I was. Though she offers to get my glasses I ask her if she'll read to me what the inscription says:

John ∞ Maureen 23.7.66

And so it is that in this final week, as though they have willed it themselves, I find, where I least expect it, proof, for better, for worse, of something true.

Afterword

When, out of the blue, Adrian received the manuscript for this book he was extremely generous, and sent his own memories. They left me sadder than I have felt in years.

My mother died just after my fifth birthday. The period is etched in my memory, trapped in a nursery school from dawn to dusk surrounded by adults who wouldn't listen to me. They wouldn't let me see her. Dad swore blind I never visited her in hospital, but I did. I will never forget seeing her lying in her bed, talking to me, reassuring me. It was the last time I ever saw her.

I never had time to grieve. I had to survive. I had to keep Dad awake on the numerous drives between Dartford and Edinburgh, standing in the front of his MG keeping lookout and stopping him from falling asleep.

Dad would never tell me about her. I tried and tried but it was harder than pulling teeth. He would never even tell me where she was buried.

Her death left me in a world full of uncaring, angry and violent adults. Granny Doyle, indifferent, smelly and uncaring, and Dad, a walking bag of rage and suppressed violence. Then Dad brought Maureen into my life. To me she was just another angry adult, much like Dad, but wearing a dress. There was no escape.

So I withdrew. You describe me as remote. An understatement if ever there was one. I withdrew into my own world of Enid Blyton and pulp children's fiction. I became so independent that I would let no one touch me. From the moment my mother went into hospital until puberty I received no affection. That was my choice.

When you and Ed came along, I changed your nappies, I read you stories, I fed you at meal times, but I never really connected with you. You were too likely to be affectionate, or even worse, need affection.

Dad had mellowed by the time you came along. You seemed to get away with stuff for which I had been soundly beaten. I resented what I saw as an 'injustice'. Of course in hindsight it was anything but.

That said, even mellowed, he was a tyrant – angry, violent and unpredictable. Life was one ginger step after another. I could never predict what would cause him to fly into a rage. It might be a word, reaching for the marmalade without asking, covering a schoolbook with paper the wrong way.

I dealt with this by spending more and more time outside, virtually coming in only to eat. Your passage about the aftermath of the burnt lino summed up my entire life from age five to sixteen. Then I fought back. He beat me up, but the balance shifted. He could no longer terrorise me.

The terror was not the beatings. I could handle those. The terror was that I never could relax. I smashed the shed window once with my football. I went in to confess and take the punishment (get it over with). He just laughed. I covered a book slightly incorrectly (simple childhood error) and was beaten so hard with a wooden spoon (the nearest weapon to hand) that it broke.

My intellect is what saved me. The only time Mum and Dad smiled at me at the same time was when I got straight As at O-grade. So when Dad tried to beat knowledge into you or Sean I would be sitting on the stairs trying to send you the answers telepathically. I really tried, but I never had the courage to come in and stop him. I could have taught you all those things, but I was too scared. In my imaginary castle, I came to the sorry conclusion that I could not trust anyone, so I drew up the metaphorical drawbridge and posted a big fuck-off sign – STAY AWAY. I was only six or seven years old.

Now I have too much good in my life to think about the past. Why dwell on all that? What's the point? They were shit parents. It happens. I survived and have done my best to fix myself. Anyway life is not about the past. It's not really about the future either. It's what we do today.

Acknowledgements

Thank you to Anna Webber for your confidence and your trust, and to Mitzi Angel. It was a privilege to work from your edit. Thank you too to everyone else at Faber: Emmie Francis, Samantha Matthews, Eleanor Rees and Camilla Smallwood for your thoughtfulness and patience. To Donna Payne, I adore your cover design – as perfect an expression of self as any of the words inside.

Thank you to my brothers. You're heroic – the material has been amazing, and your generosity too. I am more grateful than I can express.

Raquel Bello, Flora Franklin, Victoria Izat and Jennifer Ouvaroff for being such good friends, and allowing me to make you characters in this desperate book.

Bee Wilson and Annabel Lee, my first readers. Your reaction was as good as gold. Without you I'd still be writing in secret fib by fib.

Nick Barraclough and Tony Goryn for being there each week. Working with you has been remarkable, and always, always fun.

Kate Rhodes for your unstinting support and faith, to Andrea Porter for reading this twice in only a few days, flattering it with the words: 'this is fuck central', and your fabulous poker chip analogy, to Sally Fenn for your honest and empathetic feedback, which made everything better, to Malachi McIntosh for giving me the courage to send out and to Jane Menczer for travelling this road together with me.

Thank you to dear friend Katherine Davies, to Dylan Banarse and Marc Ridyard for sharing with me your views on cheating, and to my colleagues in the Kouzarides and Miska Labs, who very kindly took the Gur/Sackeim test of shame. To Dr Clive Simmonds for revealing the secret of the university library's red crates and to Pamela Bradshaw for her time and her tissues.

Thank you to Norman, for being a friend and surrogate older man of Leith these past twenty-seven years, and to Judy Eggington for talking with me about the past.

Emma and Holly Hodgson, Barbara and Stuart Mitchell, Nicola Armstrong and Vanessa Stefanak, thank you all for your belief and generosity.

Thank you Blake Morrison, Maura Dooley for an amazing two years at Goldsmiths, and Sally Cline, for opening the lid on what a hoax autobiography is.

To Arts Council England, who years ago treated me like a writer when I was still up to my ears in nappies and blaaah.

To Mark Thomson for putting the fear of God into me about privacy law.

And finally to Matthias, you are the best kind of reader and the best kind of friend. Thank you for taking me on. As Mum predicted, you have been everything. And to my children, I promise not to ever write like this about you.

Sources

Epigraph: William Maxwell, *So Long, See You Tomorrow*, London: Harvill Press (1980).

Lie 2: I am lying

4 *more than 25 per cent*: The Innocence Project, *False Confessions or Admissions*, http://www.innocenceproject.org/causes/false-confessions-admissions/.

5 *the bigger the brain*: Byrne, R. W., and Corp, N., 'Neocortex size predicts deception rates in primates', *Proceedings of the Royal Society: Biological Sciences* 271, 1549 (2004), 1693–9.

5 *the average person*: Meyer, P., *Liespotting: Proven Techniques to Detect Deception*, Macmillan: St Martin's Press (2011).

5 *Women are more likely*: Feldman, R. S., Forrest, J. A., and Happ, B. R., 'Self-presentation and Verbal Deception: Do Self-presenters Lie More?', *Basic and Applied Social Psychology* 24 (2002), 163–70.

6 *structural brain abnormalities*: Yang, Y., Raine, A., Narr, K., Lencz, T., LaCasse, L., Colletti, P., and Toga, A., 'Localisation of Increased Prefrontal White Matter in Pathological Liars', *Psychiatry: Interpersonal and Biological Processes* 190 (2007), 174–5.

6 *'leakage'*: Ekman, P., and Friesen, W. V., 'Nonverbal Leakage and Clues to Deception', *Psychiatry: Interpersonal and Biological Processes* 32, 1 (1969), 88–106.

7 *A study in 2009*: Porter, S., ten Brinke, L., and Wilson, K., 'Crime Profiles and Conditional Release Performance of Psychopathic and Non-psychopathic Sexual Offenders', *Legal and Criminological Psychology* 14, 1 (2009), 109–118.

7 *asked 110 people*: Kelly, A., and Wang, L., *A Life without Lies: How Living Honestly Can Affect Health*, APA 120th Annual Convention, Orlando, Florida, USA (2012), 32.

7 *Liars also make*: Wright, G. R. T., Berry, C. J., and Bird, G., 'Deceptively Simple . . . The "Deception-general" Ability and the Need to Put the Liar under the Spotlight', *Frontiers in Neuroscience* (2013), doi: 10.3389/fnins.2013.00152.

8 *'epic, patronising tosser'*: Rawlinson, K., 'Boris Johnson: Tony Blair Is an "Epic Tosser" for Warning against EU Vote', *Guardian*, 12 April 2015.

Lie 7: Memoir is non-fiction

22 *morally suspect*: Hardwig, J., 'Autobiography, Biography and Narrative Ethics' in H. Lindemann Nelson (ed.), *Stories and their Limits: Narrative Approaches to Bioethics*, London: Routledge (1998).

22 *'disgorged'*: Genzlinger, N., 'The Problem with Memoirs', *New York Times*, 28 January 2011, http://www.nytimes.com/2011/01/30/books/review/Genzlinger-t.html?pagewanted=all&_r=0.

23 *convince a quarter*: Loftus, E., 'Creating False Memories', *Scientific American* 277, 3 (1997), 70–5.

Lie *10:* He married well

31 *authentic personalities*: Canossa, A., El-Nasr, M. S., Colvin, R., North Eastern University, Virtual Personality Assessment Laboratory (V-PAL), http://www.northeastern.edu/games/virtual-personality-assessment-laboratory-v-pal/.

32 *a darkened room*: Barnes, C. M., et al., 'Morning People are Less Ethical at Night', *Harvard Business Review*, 23 June 2014.

32 *a bigger car*: Konnikova, M., 'Inside the Cheater's Mind', *New Yorker*, 31 April 2013.

32 *reputation to maintain*: Fu, G., et al., 'Young Children with a Positive Reputation to Maintain are Less Likely to Cheat', *Developmental Science* (2015), doi. 10.1111/desc.12304.

33 *evening the score*: Carey, B., 'The Psychology of Cheating', *New York Times*, 16 April 2011.

Lie *11:* We've posted you a present

33 *psychopathy checklist*: Schroeder, M. L., Schroeder, K. G., and Hare, R. D., 'Generalizability of a Checklist for Assessment of Psychopathy', *Journal of Consulting and Clinical Psychology* 51, 4 (August 1983), 511–6.

Lie *13:* I'm the most hard-done-by

38 *It is not what happens*: Rowe, D., 'The Sibling Bond', *Psychologies*, April 2007, https://www.psychologies.co.uk/family/the-sibling-bond.html.

39 *53 per cent*: Conley, D., *The Pecking Order: A Bold New Look at How Family and Society Determine Who We Become*, New York: Vintage (2005).

40 *Philosophers draw a line*: Bok, S., *Lying: Moral Choice in Public and Private Life*, London: Harvester Press Ltd (1978).

40 *studies of ten memories*: Sheen, M., et al., 'Disputes over Memory Ownership: What Memories Are Disputed', *Genes, Brain and Behavior* 5 (2006) (Suppl. 1), 9–13.

41 *Rowe*: Rowe, D., *My Dearest Enemy, My Dangerous Friend: Making and Breaking Sibling Bonds*, London: Routledge (2007), 66.

Lie 17: I've lost my mother

52 *programmed to attach*: Harlow, H. F., 'The Nature of Love', *American Psychologist* 13 (1958), 673–85.

Lie 18: The man will come with big scissors . . .

55 *Fifty-seven per cent*: 'Infidelity Statistics' (sources: Associated Press, *Journal of Marital and Family Therapy*), http://www.statisticbrain.com/infidelity-statistics/.

56 *omitted the word*: Molloy, C. 'Dublin Abuse Report Asks: "When Is a Lie Not a Lie?"', *National Catholic Reporter*, 1 December 2009, https://www.ncronline.org/news/accountability/dublin-abuse-report-asks-when-lie-not-lie.

Lie 21: I didn't peek at Barney

63 *bladder control*: Wong, S., 'The Lies We Tell Are More Convincing When We Need to Pee'. *New Scientist*, 19 September 2015.

64 *Barney*: Evans, A. D., et al., 'When All the Signs Point to You: Lies Told in the Face of Evidence'. *Developmental Psychology* 47, 1 (January 2011), 39–49.

65 *Dorothy Rowe*: Rowe, D., *Why We Lie*, London: Fourth Estate (2010), 50.

65 *lost shoe*: Fu, G., et al., 'Children Trust People Who Lie to Benefit Others', *Journal for Experimental Child Psychology* 128 (January 2015), 127–39.

Lie 26: I am your father

82 *stressed-out animal*: Gapp, K., et al., 'Implication of Sperm RNAs in Transgenerational Inheritance of the Effects of Early Trauma in Mice', *Nature Neuroscience* 17 (2014), 667–9.

82 *genes of the survivors' offspring*: Yehuda, R., et al., 'Influences of Maternal and Paternal PTSD on Epigenetic Regulation of the Glucocorticoid Receptor Gene in Holocaust Survivor Offspring', *American Journal of Psychiatry* 1, 8 (2014), 872–80.

82 *more significant impact on men*: Frederick, D. A., and Fales, M. R., 'Upset over Sexual vs Emotional Infidelity among Gay, Lesbian, Bisexual and Heterosexual Adults', *Archives of Sexual Behavior* (2014).

83 *'evil'*: Warnock, M., *Making Babies: Is There a Right to Have Children?*, Oxford: Oxford University Press (2002).

84 *a correlation*: Slepian, M. L., Masicampo, E. J., Toosi, N. R., and Ambady, N., 'The Physical Burdens of Secrecy', *Journal of Experimental Psychology: General* 141, 4 (2012), 619–24.

Lie 29: We're staying together for the children

91 *over 44 per cent*: Review Legal, 'Top Five Causes of Divorce and Separation in UK', 12 December 2015, http://www.reviewlegal. co.uk/about-separation-and-divorce/top-5-causes-of-divorce- and-separation.

91 *giving birth to a daughter*: Hamoudi, A., and Nobles, J., 'Do Daughters Really Cause Divorce? Stress, Pregnancy and Family Composition', *Demography* 41, 4 (2014), 1423–49.

91 *the reason people most often give*: 'Divorce Study Shows Couples Are Unhappy, But Too Scared to Split', *Huffington Post*, 18 July 2013, http://www.huffingtonpost.com/2013/07/18/divorce- study_n_3618509.html.

Lie 31: I forgot

98 *Clive Wearing*: Sacks, O., 'Abyss', *New Yorker*, 24 September 2007.

99 *One review paper*: Reardon, S., 'Drugs Help to Clear Traumatic Memories', *Nature* (2014), doi:10.1038/nature.2014.14534.

99 *a more difficult compromise*: Ackerman, S., '41 Men Targeted But 1,147 People Killed: US Drone Strikes – the Facts on the Ground', *Guardian*, 14 November 2014.

99 *'We live by leaving behind.'*: Borges, J. L., 'Funes, the Memorious', *La Nación* (1942).

100 *'nonstop, uncontrollable and automatic'*: Parker, E. S., Cahill, L., and McGaugh, J. L., 'A Case of Unusual Autobiographical Remembering', *Neurocase* 12, 1 (2006), 35–49.

100 *'strong forgetting'*: Roediger, H., Weinstein, Y., and Agarwal, P. K., 'Forgetting: Preliminary Considerations' in S. Della Salla (ed.), *Forgetting*, Hove: Psychology Press (2010).

Lie 36: I have never enjoyed taking a poo

114 *'Self-deception'*: Levine, T. R. (ed.), *Encyclopedia of Deception*, Los Angeles: Sage (2014).

114 *94 per cent*: Trivers, R., *Deceit and Self Deception*, London: Penguin Books (2011).

115 *strangers to ourselves*: Stanford Encyclopedia of Philosophy (2012), http://plato.stanford.edu/entries/self-deception/.

115 *two contradictory beliefs*: RadioLab, 'Lying to Ourselves', 16 October 2015, http://www.radiolab.org/story/91618-lying-to-ourselves/.

116 *tend to be clinically depressed*: Leslie, I., *Born Liars*, London: Quercus (2011), 202.

116 *'Have you ever wanted to rape, or be raped?'*: Gur, R. C., and Sackeim, H. A., 'Self-deception: A Concept in Search of a Phenome-

non', *Journal of Personality and Social Psychology* 37 (1979), 147–69.

117 *Joanna Starek*: Starek, J. E., and Keating, C. F., 'Self-Deception and Its Relationship to Success in Competition', *Basic and Applied Social Psychology* 12, 2 (1991).

118 *'I much fear'*: *Confessions of Saint Augustine*, trans. Edward B. Pusey, Oxford: J. H. Parker (1853), Book Ten, Chapter XXXVII.

Lie 42: That was entirely inappropriate

135 *'place cells'*: Moser, E. I., et al., 'Place Cells, Grid Cells, and the Brain's Representation System', *Annual Review of Neuroscience* 31 (2008), 69–89, doi: 10.1146/annurev.neuro.31.061307.090723.

135 *'mental travel'*: The Nobel Prize, 'Scientific Background: The Brain's Navigational Place and Grid Cell System', (2014), http://www.nobelprize.org/nobel_prizes/medicine/laureates/2014/advanced-medicineprize2014.pdf.

135 *London cab drivers*: Carr, N., 'Think Smarter with Nicholas Carr: Welcome to Nowheresville', The Penguin Blog (2015), http://penguinblog.co.uk/2015/01/27/think-smarter-with-nicholas-carr-welcome-to-nowheresville/.

136 *225 innocent people*: Loftus, E., *How Reliable Is Your Memory?* TED talk, June 2013, https://www.ted.com/talks/elizabeth_loftus_the_fiction_of_memory

Lie 44: It won't happen to my child

142 *corporate deceit*: Eisenstein, C., 'The Ubiquitous Matrix of Lies', 7 May 2007, http://charleseisenstein.net/the-ubiquitous-matrix-of-lies/.

143 *70 per cent*: 'Donald Trump's file', http://www.politifact.com/personalities/donald-trump/, accessed 7 November 2016. (70 per cent is the total of statements deemed 'mostly false' (19 per cent),

'false' (34 per cent) and 'pants on fire' (17 per cent) on Politifact's scorecard for Trump.)

143 *put into care*: Schaverien, J., 'Boarding School Syndrome: Broken Attachments – a Hidden Trauma', *British Journal of Psychiatry* 27, 2 (2011), 138–55.

143 *to avoid the humiliation*: Duffell, N., *The Making of Them*, London: Lone Arrow Press (2010).

144 *Rannoch School*: 'School may face lawsuit over sex attack', *Scotsman*, 9 September 2002, http://www.scotsman.com/news/school-may-face-lawsuit-over-sex-attack-1-620032.

145 *Sixty-two leading independent schools*: Levy, A., 'Teachers at Dozens of Leading Public Schools, Including Eton and Marlborough, implicated in Child Sex Abuse Cases', *Mail Online*, 20 January 2014, http://www.dailymail.co.uk/news/article-2542557/Teachers-dozens-leading-public-schools-including-Eton-Marlborough-implicated-child-sex-abuse-cases.html.

145 *sacked its maths teacher*: Hull, Liz, 'Boarding School Teacher Escapes Jail for Child Porn . . .', *Mail Online*, 10 February 2014, http://www.dailymail.co.uk/news/article-2555510/Boarding-school-teacher-escapes-jail-child-porn-caught-images-laptop.html

145 *abuse allegations*: Renton, A., 'Rape, Child Abuse and Prince Charles's Former School', *Observer*, 12 April 2015.

145 *'I can't think of any'*: Tickle, L., 'Britain's Elite Boarding Schools Are Facing an Explosion of Abuse Allegations', *Newsweek*, 1 September 2014.

Lie 46: Jesus knows best

149 *Our self-story*: McAdams, D. P., 'The Psychology of Life Stories', *Review of General Psychology* 5, 2 (2001), 100–22.

150 *'chief fictional character'*: Dennett, D., 'The Self as the Centre of Narrative Gravity' in F. Kessel et al. (eds). *Self and Consciousness: Multiple Perspectives*, Hillsdale NJ: Erbam (1992).

Lie 49: I deserved it

157 *'It is always for the prosecution'*: Rights of Women, *From Court to Report* (2014).

157 *cited by Lord Falconer*: HL Deb 31 March 2003 vol 646 cc1048-110 *Hansard*, http://hansard.millbanksystems.com/lords/2003/mar/31/sexual-offences-bill-hl#column_1048

158 *convictions have increased*: the conviction rate in 2001–2, according to Lord Falconer in the Lords debate, was 5.8 per cent of recorded allegations and 45 per cent of those charged (ibid.); in 2015–16 it was 7.5 per cent of recorded allegations and 57.9 per cent of those charged (Dodd, Vikram, and Bengtsson, Helena, 'Reported Rapes in England and Wales Double in Four Years', https://www.theguardian.com/society/2016/oct/13/reported-rapes-in-england-and-wales-double-in-five-years).

158 *26 per cent*: 'Police Fail to Record One in Five Crimes Reported to Them, Says Report', 16 November 2014, www.bbc.co.uk/news/uk-30081682.

Lie 55: Honestly it won't be so bad

179 *Large pills*: Leslie, I., *Born Liars: Why We Can't Live without Deceit*, London: Quercus (2011).

179 *Ninety-three per cent*: Howick, J., et al., 'Placebo Use in the UK: Results of a National Survey of Primary Care Practitioners' (2013), PLoS One, doi: 10.1371/journal.pone.0058247.

179 *two hundred patients*: Feinberg, C., 'The Placebo Phenomenon', *Harvard Magazine*, January–February 2013.

179 *seven-year-olds*: Lee, K., et al., 'White Lie-telling in Children for Politeness Purposes', *International Journal of Behavioral Development* 31, 1 (2007), 1–11.

Lie 60: Let me tell you a secret

197 *secrets are a burden*: Foster, C. A., et al., 'Are Secret Relationships Hot, Then Not?', *Journal of Social Psychology* 150, 6 (2010), 668–88.

197 *bury who we are*: Krauss Whitbourne, S., 'Why We Keep Secrets from Our Partners', *Psychology Today*, 10 June 2014, https://www.psychologytoday.com/blog/fulfillment-any-age/201406/why-we-keep-secrets-our-partners.

198 *When we become terminally ill*: Hardwig, J., 'Autobiography, Biography and Narrative Ethics' in H. Lindemann Nelson (ed.), *Stories and Their Limits: Narrative Approaches to Bioethics*, London: Routledge (1997), 54.

Lie 64: I am good

212 *'professional victim'*: Kellaway, K., 'No Pain, No Gain', *Observer*, 15 February 2004, http://www.theguardian.com/books/2004/feb/15/biography.features.

213 *two camps*: Douglas, K., *Contesting Childhood: Autobiography, Trauma and Memory*, London: Rutgers University Press (2011), 146–8

213 *what are we to do*: Howes, C., 'Afterword' in Paul John Eakin (ed.), *The Ethics of Life Writing*, London: Cornell University Press (2005), 245.

213 *Synaptic pruning*: Nelson, C. A., Bos, K., Gunnar, M. R. and Sonuga-Barke, E. J. S. , V. *The Neurobiological Toll of Early Human Deprivation*. Monographs of the Society for Research in Child De-

velopment, 76: 127–46 (2011). doi:10.1111/j.1540-5834.2011.00630.x

214 *'I was so frustrated'*: Barron, J., 'Completely without Dignity: An Interview with Karl Ove Knausgaard', *Paris Review*, 26 December 2013.

Lie 69: *It's not easy for me to do this*

229 *A paper*: Okimoto, G., Wenzel, M., and Hedrick, K., 'Refusing to Apologise Can Have Psychological Benefits', *European Journal of Social Psychology* 43, 1 (2012), doi: 10.1002/ejsp.1901.

Lie 70: *Always tell the truth*

232 *Robert Kurzban argues*: Kurzban, R., and Aktipis, C. A., 'Modularity and the Social Mind: Are Psychologists Too Self-ish?', *Personality and Social Psychology Review* 11, 2 (2007), 131–49.

233 *most prized qualities*: 'Being Human: Honesty, Respect and Tolerance', School of Advanced Study: University of London (October 2014), http://www.sas.ac.uk/about-us/news/being-human-honesty-respect-and-tolerance.

233 *In another study*: Zhu, L., et al., 'Damage to Dorsolateral Prefrontal Cortex Affects Tradeoffs between Honesty and Self-interest', *Nature Neuroscience* 17 (2014), 1319–21.

234 *never confess*: Kirshenbaum, M., *When Good People Have Affairs: Inside the Hearts and Minds of People in Two Relationships*, New York: St Martin's Press (2009).

234 *define ourselves through memory*: Apter, T., *The Sister Knot: Why We Fight, Why We're Jealous and Why We'll Love Each Other No Matter What*, London: W. W. Norton & Co. (2008).

257